Directed W
and
Readin

Directed Writing and Reading

A COURSE IN COMPOSITION AND COMPREHENSION

R. A. Banks

HODDER AND STOUGHTON

LONDON SYDNEY AUCKLAND TORONTO

For: Mary-Lou

British Library Cataloguing in Publication Data

Banks, R. A.
   Directed writing and reading: (a course
   in composition and comprehension)
   1. English language—Composition and
   exercises
   I. Title
   808'.042   PE1413
   ISBN 0 340 35695 2

First published 1985

Set in 11 on 12pt Optima by
Rowland Phototypesetting, Bury St Edmunds, Suffolk

Printed in Great Britain for
Hodder and Stoughton Educational,
a division of Hodder and Stoughton Ltd,
Mill Road, Dunton Green, Sevenoaks, Kent
by Butler & Tanner Ltd,
Frome and London

Contents

Acknowledgments

For permission to quote copyright material the authors and publishers wish to thank: Batsford Academic and Educational Ltd for an extract from *Life and Work of The People of England* by D. Hartley and M. M. Elliott; Bell & Hyman Publishers for an extract from *School Physics* by W. E. Pearce; Adam and Charles Black Publishers for an extract from *Autobook No. 763 Rover 3500 SE, U8S 1976–81* by K. Ball; British Telecom for an extract from *The Directory Section 475*, 1982, pp. 184–5 (adapted form); Curtis Brown and The Estate of Dr Bronowski for an extract from *Letters to Prosperity* by Dr Jacob Bronowsky, appearing in *The Listener*; Casio Electronics Co. Ltd for the advertisement 'We've covered the syllabus. Every syllabus!'; Cassell Ltd for an extract from *The Second World War*, Volume II by Sir Winston Churchill; Collins Publishers and A. M. Peters & Co. Ltd for an extract from *Potterism* by Rose Macaulay; Andre Deutsch Ltd for an extract from 'As I walked out one midsummer morning' by Laurie Lee; Doubleday and the Open University Press for an extract from *The Social Construction of Reality* by Peter L. Berger and Thomas Luckmann; Euroways Express Coaches Ltd for two extracts from *The Summer Timetable 1983*; Faber and Faber Ltd for the poem 'O what is that sound' from *Collected Poems* by W. H. Auden; Granada Publishing Ltd for an extract from *A Clip of Steel* by Thomas Blackburn; Hawthorn Books, Inc. for an extract from *Goebbels* by Helmut Heiber; Heinemann Educational Books for two extracts from *A New Certificate Chemistry* (pp. 308–9) by A. J. Holderness and John Lambert, 1977, 5th edition; Heinemann (William) Ltd for an extract from *Dear Me* by Peter Ustinov; David Higham Associates Ltd for an extract from *The Best of Arthur C. Clarke* by Arthur C. Clarke; Hogarth Press for an extract from *Cider with Rosie* by Laurie Lee; Tessa Le Bars Management for an extract from *Steptoe and Son* by Ray Galton and Alan Simpson; Harold Lloyd Trust for a picture of Harold Lloyd; Ward Lock Ltd for two extracts from *Mrs Beeton's Everyday Cookery*; Methuen and Co. Ltd for an extract from *Understanding News* (in the series 'Studies in Communication') by John Hartley; Vallentine Mitchell & Co. Ltd for an extract from *The Diary of Anne Frank*, 1954; John Murray for an extract from *A New Introduction to Physics* by W. Ashhurst; A. D. Peters and Co. for an extract from *Mr Loveday's Little Outing* by Evelyn Waugh; Penguin Books Ltd for approx. 650 words

Introduction

This is a book about Composition and Comprehension. It suggests and sets out an approach which encourages sound, stimulated and relevant writing and reading, and considers in detail the point of view of the writer, the topic and the context of the writing, and the reader at whom writing is directed – the 'audience'.

Much of our life is spent listening as well as seeing; part of it is spent reading and part of it talking. Much less, perhaps, is spent writing, and yet skill in writing is emphasised in school and college, since it helps us to formulate ideas and record observations and reactions across a wide range of activities. Without a well-developed skill in writing our ability to learn and our enjoyment of life are impaired.

Although writing skills are needed in very specific contexts and for very specific purposes and audiences in the study of subjects across the curriculum *in school or college*, work in English sometimes deliberately leaves topics, contexts and audiences far less specific so that the imagination can set its own limits within which to operate. This freedom often imposes great problems for young people who fall back on chewing the ends of their pens or thinking about the weekend's activities before they finally ask, 'What can I write about?' or 'How can I start?' The work too often becomes sprawling and undisciplined. Time spent in establishing the angle from which to write, the scope of the topic, the context, and the intended reader can lead to more structured, relevant and successful writing.

After school or college, as well as offering the individual man or woman activities which bring great pleasure in their own right, writing and reading are often fundamental tools at work. Signs, notices, reports, letters, minutes, and advertisements take on importance and most of us find ourselves writing and reading within very specific contexts, on very specific topics, and for very specific reasons; in writing we usually have a very clear idea about the person or group our words are aimed at.

Recent government reports, research papers, and practical teachers have often emphasised the need to write and to read within context and with a sense of audience. This book sets out, with many lively examples and exercises, to explore the range of possibilities open to the writer to choose his or her own point of view, topic, context, and audience and the ways to read with understanding and rigour texts which some other writer has directed at a particular reader. It examines the factors which help to condition narrative, discursive, descriptive, exponential and dramatic writing in the areas young people experience across the curriculum and in their daily lives. They are expected to recognise and be able to use a huge range of registers as they study Physics, Geography, History, Chemistry, Religious Studies, Home Economics and Modern Languages – as well as English Language and English Literature. This acquisition of control over language is complex but necessary.

This book suggests relevant approaches to writing and reading and suggests attitudes, questions, and opportunities throughout its explanations and exercises which will allow the sensitive teacher and student to explore the uses of English in realistic contexts. It does not aim to provide a manual of spelling, punctuation, and grammar but a source of stimulating material, in which to use these essential skills, as writing and reading are approached from the consideration of the writer's point of view, topic, context and audience. Used conscientiously and with imagination, it will provide a sound year's work in composition and comprehension for those preparing for public examinations such as GSCE, GCE, CSE, City and Guilds and RSA Certificates, which demand accurate, relevant, and stimulated writing and close, sensitive reading. It should also provide some fun.

I have benefited from talking over approaches used in this book with many practising teachers and with my wife, Mary-Lou, who has given me her usual warm encouragement throughout its preparation. I am also grateful to Mrs Daphne Meeking who has patiently deciphered my handwriting and produced a final immaculate typescript.

R.A.B.
Sunbury-on-Thames, 1984

Recognising the Signs   1

The purpose of reading and writing

We read and write for a purpose. This book will help you examine why you read and write and how the purposes affect the English you find and use; such an examination may even help you to improve the quality of your own reading and writing.

1.1

We **read**, perhaps, for pleasure, to acquire information, to educate ourselves, to escape from the humdrum world of everyday life, or to keep up with current news and developments. It is certain that we rarely read without a purpose; even the idle turning of a magazine's pages in a dentist's waiting room serves to distract our attention.

We **write**, perhaps, to communicate our thoughts and feelings to others, to express ourselves to ourselves, to pass examinations, to apply for jobs, to pay bills, to order goods, to question tax inspectors, and to declare our love for someone else. Again, it is clear that we always write with a purpose.

The purpose of our reading and writing directs them both; it leads us to choose one book rather than another and write in one kind of language rather than another. The purpose and the direction of what we read and write will determine what we understand and how we express ourselves. Both the understanding and the expression, in turn, will depend on our sensitivity to the way language operates and can be used on a number of different levels – sometimes on more than one level at the same time. Poets, for example, frequently rely on multi-level meanings to achieve their effects: in his dedication to his auto-biography, *A Clip of Steel*, Thomas Blackburn, a modern poet, wrote,

1.2

> We are such stuff as dreams are made on . . .
> SHAKESPEARE: The Tempest

In the sense of this quotation, all the characters in this book, including myself, are entirely fictitious.

It is worth considering for a moment, just how far the meaning of the word 'fictitious' can be defined; its 'ambiguous' use ('admitting more than one meaning') is its strength in this context.

1.3

Any act where language is used presupposes *four* things:

a) **A speaker**; **a writer** (the instigator).
b) **A topic** (the subject matter).
c) **A context** (the situation in which the language is used).
d) **A listener**; **a reader** (the recipient or audience).

In May 1978, the Department of Education and Science published a research document, *Language Performance*, produced by a special team set up within the National Foundation for Educational Research. Their work showed that the questions 'What do we read, and why?' and 'What do we write, and why?' are central to the way the English language is used.

> Any use of language, whether spoken or written, implies that someone is seeking to convey meaning to someone else. In other words, there is always a context, about which we can ask, 'Who is saying (or writing) what, to whom, and why?' The answers to these questions have important consequences for *what* can be said (or written) in a given context, and for *how* it can be said. Apart from the function that the language is intended to serve, the relationship between the speaker and the listener is especially significant. This is recognised in the concept of audience, *i.e.* the person (or persons) to whom an act of speech or writing is addressed.

Using correct and appropriate language

1.4

The effect of recognising that any act of language involves a speaker (or writer), a topic, a context, and a listener (or reader) and that the purpose and direction of the language are of crucial importance must lead us on to consider the ways in which language is used. Given these circumstances, 'What is correct?' 'What is appropriate?' become key questions.

1.5

The notion of **correct** English seems to imply that there is a list of rules drawn up by an all-powerful authority and that a student has only to discover, learn, and obey them in order to be able to speak or write fluently and clearly. No such list exists; the student has to learn a different approach for him or herself.

1.6

It is much more useful to recognise what is an **appropriate** form of language for a topic, within a context, for a speaker (or writer) to use in order to communicate ideas (feelings, etc.) towards a listener (or reader). Native speakers of a language quickly learn to recognise what is basically appropriate and what is basically inappropriate for a particular context, but this recognition will be increased if a student listens to, reads and studies a wide range of 'varieties' of English.

Consider carefully the following passages and say:

1.7

a) What **context** the language is appropriate for;
b) If any forms of the language used in the passage are **inappropriate** for such a context.

i) 'Birmingham. Two Awaydays.'
'International or New Street?'
'What's the difference?'
'None. For the tickets.'
'All right, New Street. What times do they go?'
'Where from?'
'Euston.'
'Ten and forty past the hour. What about him?'
'He's under five.'
'You pay the normal fare. He pays a pound.'
'Not bad, is it?'
'It can't last.'
'Thanks.'
'Thanks.'

(Are there any 'ambiguities' here?)

ii) There were 250 of us attending an extraordinary event in London called the Character Merchandising Conference. I can't remember why I went. As for merchandising, marketing and retailing, I know as much about these as I do about the digestive system of the hermit crab. My mother wanted me to be a buyer for Dorothy Perkins, but I didn't pass the test.

But I *love* conferences. I love being referred to as a delegate and hearing announcements like 'Will Mr Cyril Loveday of Chislehurst Novelty Goods and Slipwear please come to reception?' My last conference was a very serious affair in Cardiff called The International Convention on Humour and Laughter to which delegates from Swaziland and Samoa came armed with ethnic jokes and passed resolutions about banana skins . . . I have attended conferences on ferret maintenance, heavy duty floor coverings and scientology. And now I remember why I went to the seminar on Character Merchandising. It was Mickey Mouse's birthday that week. He was fifty.

iii) The system operates on the conventional thermo-syphon principle and is impeller-pump assisted. A thermostat is fitted behind the water outlet elbow at the forward end of the inlet manifold casting. This prevents coolant circulation until a pre-determined temperature is reached in the engine. On the 3500 engines the fan is mounted directly on the pump hub unit but on 3500S engines a shock-absorbing viscous drive unit is interposed between the fan and the belt-driven hub. The viscous unit cannot be repaired or adjusted and in the event of failure must be renewed completely.

(Can the language of this extract be simplified without loss or change of meaning?)

iv) Now acknowledged as one of ballet's corner-stones, the supreme test for everybody in the theatre from the prima ballerina assoluta down to the fourth assistant machinist, *Swan Lake* made a halting, botched start. The first performance at the Bolshoi, in 1877, was a benefit night for Karpakova, a dancer otherwise unknown to history. Scenery and costumes had been dug up from loft and wardrobe stocks on the 'nearest fit' principle. The music suffered a good deal of plastic surgery. Certain numbers, considered too 'symphonic' to be danceable or even agreeable, were cut out and replaced by graftings from other ballets. What was left went in at one ear and went out at the other. *Swan Lake* was much too big and riotously varied a conception to be properly assessed by the contemporary Russian ballet-goer, who had been nurtured on the smallest of small musical beer.

(Look at the vocabulary and idioms carefully here.)

v) You are entitled to drive provided that you can meet the conditions specified below.
Section 84(4) of the Road Traffic Act 1972, as amended, permits a person to drive vehicles of any class, despite the fact that he does not actually hold a driving licence, provided that:

    a) he has previously held a licence to drive those vehicles and is still entitled to obtain one (i.e. he is not disqualified, or the licence would not be or has not been refused on medical grounds)

    b) a valid application for the grant of a licence has been received at the Driver and Vehicle Licensing Centre and

    c) any conditions which apply when using that licence, such as those applicable to provisional licence holders, are met.

This section allows a person to drive without actually holding the licence for a period of not more than one year from the date of receipt of the application, but does not apply once the licence is issued.

Look carefully at the qualifications to the main statements here.)

Register and style

The word **register** is sometimes used to refer to the level on which spoken or written English is used. There is no easy way of defining one 'register' rather than another and there can be no suggestion that registers are discrete or always apply to one context and one context only. Nevertheless, the language of insurance policies or court procedures, of commerce and of journalism, of computer-studies or of economics is clearly recognisable. The sensitive user of language will have a range of registers which he or she can bring to bear on a particular context. If an inappropriate register is married to an inappropriate context, the effect will jar or embarrass.

Writers of plays and novels frequently use this discordant marriage of inappropriate register and context to amuse their audiences. Shakespeare makes Dogberry (in *Much Ado about Nothing*) try to speak above his station; as a result he appears a pompous buffoon. Similarly, it is interesting to compare the ways Dickens makes Joe Gargery talk to Pip, first as a boy and then later as a successful gentleman (Chapters 7 and 27 of *Great Expectations*); he adapts his way of speaking, fights to discover words, prolongs his pronunciation of them to appear polite; even his accent changes, quite inappropriately:

'Pip, how AIR you, Pip?'

The greater a student's awareness of 'register' appropriate to contexts, the greater will be his or her effectiveness in using the English language in speech or writing. Success in directing the language at an audience depends on the ability to change and adapt register according to context.

Style arises from the choice of language arising from a response to all the elements that make up 'context'. Most native users of the language can easily adapt their 'style' of speaking and writing to match the topic, the context, and the audience.

If the speaker or writer knows the audience well, the language between them may be relaxed and friendly, not particularly detailed or specific – partly because they will share common knowledge or expertise. At one extreme of such an intimate kind of language there may be the familiar language used by husband and wife, sweethearts and close friends; at the other extreme lies *jargon*, a trade dialect used by groups such as doctors, teachers, carpenters, etc., which is economical, precise, and accurate in its use. If the speaker or writer does not know his audience well, then since they do not share common knowledge or experience, the language will become formal, stiff, impersonal, and usually very explicit.

1.10

Consider, for example, the 'styles' of the following passages: *informal, formal,* and *neutral*. The style will have been determined by **topic**, **context** and **audience**. Decide what these are and say what the main features of each of the styles are.

a) Informal

ALBERT   You're late, ain't you?

HAROLD   Am I? Oh, I've been so busy I haven't had a chance to think about the time.

ALBERT   It's gone half past seven. How long have you been out? I didn't hear you go this morning.

HAROLD   No, well, I thought I'd get an early start. Get our cards poked through the doors, then call back round again. You know, before the other lads get started, get all the best stuff.

ALBERT   You have worked hard, haven't you?

HAROLD   Well, you know . . .

ALBERT   You've got a lot of stuff here.
         They start to unload the cart.

HAROLD   Yes, not bad. Should make us about ten quid. That's two weeks' rent for the room, isn't it? (Casually) Have you had any enquiries for the room yet?

ALBERT   No, not yet.

HAROLD   Haven't you really? I would have thought they would have been round like flies round a dustbin, the housing situation being what it is.

ALBERT   Don't worry. It's early days yet. They'll be round.
         (ALBERT *takes a kilt off the cart, out of a sack.*)

ALBERT   Here, this is good, ain't it?

HAROLD   That's a real kilt, that is. That's a Scots one, that is. That's the Hunting Stewart. Yards of material in that, you know.

ALBERT   I fought with this lot in the fourteen–eighteen war. Women from hell, the Germans called them. I have my photograph taken in one of these, you know. Have you seen the photo of me in a kilt?

HAROLD   Oh yes, very sexy.

ALBERT   Course, I had better knees in them days.

b) Formal

The skull is supported on the summit of the vertebral column, and is of an oval shape, wider behind than in front. It is composed of a series of flattened or irregularly shaped bones which, with one exception (the lower jaw), are immovably joined together. It is divided into two parts, the Cranium and the Face, the former of which constitutes a case for the accommodation and protection of the brain, while opening on the face are the orifices of the nose and mouth: between the cranium above and the face below the orbital cavities are situated. The Cranium (χράνος, a helmet) is composed of eight bones. The Face is composed of fourteen bones.

Between these extremes lies a whole range of styles along a continuum. Consider, for example, the following passage of an autobiography by Richard Church. Its style is literary and personal, but it is not 'informal' and has not the fixed jargon of 'formal' English. The area of style between the two extremes has sometimes been called **neutral**, but such a term denies non-informal and non-formal styles their own particular qualities – which are often very distinct:

c) Neutral

Then one day a gaunt young man with long hair and a nervous cough came to tune the piano. I noticed his thin, dirty hands, with finger-nails like claws, that rattled on the keys and scratched the face board behind them. He smoked cigarettes the whole time he was at work: and that was an unusual habit in 1900.

Jack and I were vastly interested. We stood side by side watching him that Saturday morning. He took out the front of the piano, exposing the strings and the rusty pegs. That was wonderful enough. But he talked to us while he worked, breaking off the conversation at intervals while he struck a note and called forth a clank from the three strings whose neighbours had been muted by a metal tool stuck through them. He talked to Jack, over my head, and my attention wandered.

Exercises

The first chapter showed that writing (or speaking) and reading have to take into account *four* main elements:

1   Who is writing (or speaking) – the writer (or speaker);
2   What is he or she writing (or speaking) about – the topic;
3   What is the situation or what are the set of circumstances for which the writing (or speaking) is intended or being used in – the context;
4   Who is being addressed – the audience.

Directed reading

1   Read the following extracts in order to establish for each:

   a) Who the *probable writer* was (A man or woman? Age? Profession/Job? Position? Relation to the 'audience'?).
   b) *The topic* (Try to state this in about twenty words).
   c) *The context* (Keep your comments as brief as possible).
   d) *The audience* (A man or woman? Age? An individual or a small/large group? Relationship to the 'writer'?).

   i)   Remember modern printing equipment unavoidably loses a tiny strip around edges of negative. Always keep important subjects well within frame of viewfinder. We take every care of your property. All photographic materials are accepted on the basis that their value does not exceed the cost of the material. Responsibility is limited to the replacement of film. No liability will be accepted consequential or otherwise however caused. Any other warranties express or implied are excluded. Any statutory rights are not affected.
         Our aim is to ensure that benefits are continuously derived from advances in photographic technology and techniques. We therefore reserve the right to alter specifications, finishes, and materials without prior notice.

   ii)

My fiancé is kind, loving and generous – I can't find any fault with him – but I feel terribly trapped. We're both still young and in the three years we've known each other I've lost all my friends and we don't mix with anyone except his family and mine. Sometimes I feel I'd like to go out with other lads. But I know I couldn't find a nicer one and he'd be very hurt if I broke with him, even for a month or so to see how it worked out. What can I do?

iii)

iv) Pure carbon is found in the form of diamond (India, South Africa) and impure carbon as a graphite (Sri Lanka). Carbon is a constituent of numerous naturally occurring substances such as coal, mineral oils, carbonates, organic matter of all kinds and occurs in the air to a small but very important extent ($\cdot$03–$\cdot$04% by volume) as carbon dioxide.

Carbon is not a very reactive substance chemically. All forms of carbon can be made to burn in excess of oxygen to form carbon dioxide, although the temperature at which they commence to burn varies. As the carbon burns a great amount of heat is liberated.

Owing to the fact that carbon combines readily with oxygen, it acts as a reducing agent and is used in industrial practice in obtaining iron and zinc from their ores.

v) Alex 'Hurricane' Higgins stoked up a storm at the world snooker championship in Sheffield last night. Boiling point came when the defending champion claimed opponent Willie Thorne had played a deliberate miss in their second round match.

Said Thorne after the session: 'Alex called me a cheat. He said I would stab my own grandmother for two bob.'

Higgins, who ended the opening session 5–3 ahead, insisted: 'I never called Willie a cheat but I did tell him that I thought he'd stab his grandmother for two bob. He deliberately missed that shot, but I know there are people who would be willing to kill to take the world championship away from me.

'I'm the one who's here to kill and that's exactly what I intend to do.'

vi) I was confronted by fifty expressionless boys at a school famous for its military associations. At the end of my talk and reading, no questions were forthcoming from those overdisciplined creatures. But Mr Glazier, the Senior English Master, stepped into the breach.

'Do you,' he inquired earnestly, 'write more poems in the Spring?'

'Do you imagine that I am a crocus or a sparrow?'

There was a wan titter. But Mr Glazier was distressed. A fond illusion had gone.

'But I thought poets always wrote more in the Spring,' he murmured sadly.

vii)

Bring home everything with ease

Bring home everything with ease. The detachable front basket is just right for the family shopping and the large capacity rear holdall with carrying strap doubles as a smart shoulder bag. Parking is so simple too with the neat, kick-down prop-stand. There's a super-comfort mattress saddle and deep section, weather protective mudguards. Saddle and handle-bar heights are quickly adjustable to suit almost anyone . . .

   No shopping bags to weight you down, no bus queues to hold you up, no parking restrictions to move you on – the 'Shopper' makes fun of shopping. There is a Sturmey-Archer 3-speed gear hub and handlebar twistgrip gear change.

viii) It is usually best to go for the set menu for the day – the one posted outside on the card held up by cut-out figures of high-hatted, plump chefs or of strutting cockerels about to jump into the road. These menus often include service-and-wine, too, if you're lucky. Most restaurants offer you an à *la carte* service, if you have time to wait. A good three- or four-course meal can cost as little as £5 of less – a starter, a main dish and a sweet or cheese.

    Watch where the lorry-drivers pull up exactly at mid-day if you want to find a good café with excellent food at reasonable prices. Don't expect luxurious surroundings but the service will be quick and very efficient. If you feel you must use more comfortable restaurants, what you will get for £10 per head will far out-do what you can find in a similar restaurant in England.

    Why not take a picnic for the mid-day meal? Fresh crusty

bread, a slice of delicious meat from the local *charcuterie* or a piece of French cheese just ready for eating, with a juicy peach to round things off provide a cheap and nutritious meal. Even the local cows are friendly!

ix) One of the best ways of simplifying the actual clerical work of keeping accounts is to shop always with a written list of requirements. Hand the list to the shopkeeper, who will make out the order and return the list with prices written in. Accounting need not be complicated; in the small household a simple small notebook will suffice. What *is* essential is that each and every expenditure should be noted down, and the balance struck at least once a week.

Careful scrutiny of her accounts nearly always prompts the conscientious but inexperienced housewife to ask herself, 'Am I getting the best value for money? Should I buy different things, or shop elsewhere?' Obviously the answers to these questions will vary with different women and in different circumstances. Careful shopping can save a lot of money, but it can also take a lot of time which might, perhaps, be better used in some other way.

x) A deep depression will persist W of Britain. 6 am to midnight.
London, East Anglia, Midlands: Showers, some heavy, perhaps hail and thunder, bright intervals; wind S, fresh or strong; max 12 or 13C (54 or 55F).
SE: SW and Central S England, Wales, Channel Islands: Showers, heavy and prolonged in places, perhaps hail and thunder, some bright intervals; wind mainly SW, fresh or strong, locally gale in exposed parts; max 10 to 12C (50 to 54F).
Lake District, Borders, E, NE, NW and Central N England, SW Scotland, N Ireland: Showers, heavy and prolonged at times, perhaps hail and thunder, some bright intervals; wind mainly SE, fresh or strong, locally gale in exposed parts; max 10 to 12C (50 to 54F).
Edinburgh, Dundee, Aberdeen, Glasgow, Central Highlands: Showers, some heavy and prolonged, bright intervals, wind mainly E, fresh or strong, locally gale in exposed parts; max 8 to 11C (48 to 52F).
Moray Firth, Argyll, NW Scotland: Sunny intervals, scattered showers; wind E, fresh or strong, locally gale in exposed parts; max 9 to 12C (48 to 54F).
NE Scotland, Orkney, Shetlands: Bright intervals, scat-

tered showers; wind E, strong or gale; max 8 to 10C (46 to 50F).

Outlook for tomorrow and Friday: Staying unsettled, heavy showers at times. Temperatures becoming nearer normal.

SEA PASSAGES: North Sea: Wind fresh or strong, locally gale at times; sea mainly rough. **Straits of Dover, English Channel (E), St. George's Channel:** Wind SW, strong, occasionally gale; sea rough or very rough. **Irish Sea:** wind S, fresh or strong, locally gale at times; sea mainly rough.

2 Take *one* of the passages given in the Directed Reading exercise above (pp. 8–13) and find the answers to the following questions:

   a) What point of view does the writer take up? How can you tell?

   b) What is the relationship between the *writer* and the *audience*? What gives this relationship away? Is it implied or is it explicit?

   c) What is there in the choice of words to indicate the writer's intention and the *context*?

   d) Are there any features of the writing to help you decide the level on which the *writer* expects his *audience* to take it? What are these features? Does the writer succeed?

   e) Comment on the *topic* of the passage? What details have been selected? How have they been arranged?

   f) What is the evidence in the passage itself that it is presented in 'written' English rather than 'speech'? Could the passage (or parts of it) be re-presented as dialogue? If so, what changes in the language would have to be made?

3 Imagine that you have sent an exposed film of an important family occasion (e.g. a wedding, a holiday, a visit to a grandmother who has since died) which can never be repeated for developing and printing to the company whose comments formed Passage (i) in the Directed Reading Exercise above (p. 8). The prints have been returned but only two have come out clearly; the company has disclaimed all responsibility for the results. Write a letter to the Managing Director expressing your disappointment, asking for a check on their processing procedures, and demanding compensation. (Set out your work in a formal letter and be careful to present your arguments clearly, to establish and maintain an appropriate level of writing, and to try to persuade the Managing Director to take positive and sympathetic action.)

4 Compose a suitable reply to the letter set out as Passage (*ii*) in the Directed Reading Exercise above (p. 8). Use an appropriate level

of writing once you have established your own viewpoint as the writer, the subject-matter you wish to include, the context in which you are writing, and the person for whom your reply is intended. (Some of the matters you will have to consider are: How far should I tell another person what to do? How sympathetic should I be? What is the writer of the letter really asking? How can I be tactful and yet helpful? How can I avoid seeming to be 'superior' or 'hard' or 'amused'?)

5   Bearing in mind the level and style of writing appropriate to the task, write a report for a member of the science staff of your school or college of an experiment in Chemistry *or* Physics *or* Biology you have done recently in your spare time. (You must take special care over your arrangement of the *topic* material; you may draw a diagram if this will help your written report.)

6   Imagine that you have recently been to a sporting event (a football or hockey match, an athletics meeting, a gymkhana or a concert) which was marred by the bad behaviour of a section of the crowd. Write a letter to a popular national tabloid newspaper deploring the trend of a few trying to spoil the pleasure of many by their disruptive attitudes. (Use an appropriate form and style so that the editor can re-produce your letter in his column without having to alter anything.)

7   Examine carefully Passage (*vi*) in the Directed Reading Exercise above (p. 10). Then write an entry that Mr Glazier, the Senior English Master, might have written for his own personal diary following the school's poetry reading. (Establish clearly in your own mind before you begin whether the diary is intended only for your own interest or for later publication and whether you intend to place the emphasis on a factual report or on comment.)

8   Examine carefully Passage (*vii*) in the Directed Reading Exercise above (p. 10). Then write a letter to the sales director of the bicycle firm to express your approval of the product they advertise but commenting on their implicit assumption that it is only women who should do the family shopping. (You may write as a boy or girl, man or woman, and may compliment or attack the company about their assumption and the general tone of their advertising copy. Present your views in a controlled and appropriate manner and make your own viewpoint and stance clear; bear in mind that you are asking the sales director to re-consider the way he presents his company's product to the public.)

9   Write a tongue-in-cheek report for a serious national newspaper of a discussion between politicians or between sportsmen you have watched and listened to recently on television. (This is a difficult

exercise in which you must strike a happy balance between fact, reporting of the fact and comment; assume that your *audience* is sensitive enough to pick up easily your sense of humour – which need not, therefore, be laboured or excessive.)

10 Basing your writing on the weather report you heard last night on television or on radio and on your observation of today's weather, re-present the report (with the benefit of hindsight) as it should have been given had its forecasts been totally accurate. (You may, if you wish, model your weather report on the style of a presenter who appears regularly on television or radio; bear in mind your 'audience', some who will be sceptical but many who may be seeking reassurance as well as the facts about the next day's weather.)

11 Compose an accurate piece of directed writing, using an appropriate format, style, and level of meaning in accordance with the following data:

    The writer   : You
    The topic   : A letter breaking a piece of very bad news.
    The context   : A letter received from abroad; after an absence of two weeks, you know your letter will produce first pleasure and then anguish.
    The audience : Your family, happy that you have been able to get away for a well-deserved holiday.

12 Continue the following passage of dialogue; keep to the main topic but develop the situation, observe the relationship between the speakers, and maintain an appropriate level of language which takes account of the context:

    GAIL : Why did you ask me out, then?
    MIKE : I thought you would enjoy the match. After all, Yorkshire don't play here every week. Do you know, last time they came to the Oval . . .?
    GAIL : Oh, no! Not that again! Can't we go to the Wimpy Bar and then on the disco?
    MIKE : Did you see that? That ball should have taken his off-stump out!
    GAIL : I thought Sean looked great yesterday. He's keen on Julie, d'you know?

2 The Personal Point of View

Determining the writer's point of view

This chapter and **Chapters 3** and **4** deal with the role of the writer (or speaker) in the act of communication. The point of view he or she adopts will be determined to a large degree by the other elements in the act: *topic, context,* and *audience.*

2.1 Emily Brontë's novel *Wuthering Heights* (published in 1847) presented an intense, romantic story of passion and cruelty set in a wild, rugged landscape. It is interesting stylistically because the story is presented from a number of different points of view:

a) *The **personal** point of view (using narrative):* the story begins with an account written in the first person ('I') of visits by a Mr Lockwood to 'Wuthering Heights'.

b) *The **dramatic** point of view:* the events unfold themselves almost immediately through direct speech (dialogue), when Mr Lockwood meets Heathcliff, his landlord and one of the two major characters in the book.

c) *The **objective** point of view (using commentary):* the background to the present situation is given to Mr Lockwood by an old servant, Mrs Dean. She acts as a reporter, now standing outside the main story but free to comment and to arrange the events as she sees fit. Sometimes she uses narrative in the first person ('I', 'we'); sometimes she uses direct speech (dialogue) and sometimes indirect speech (reported conversation); sometimes she uses a more objective style of narrative in the third person ('he', 'she', 'it', 'they'). Her *point of view*, however, remains that of someone now outside the main events and acting as a reporter. Her account forms the main plot of the novel, although Emily Brontë re-introduces the personal narrative of Mr Lockwood and dramatic dialogue from time to time to change the perspective.

2.2 Often, however, novelists and other writers prefer to adopt a more disinterested role, where they stand completely outside the main events and report or present them at a distance. This point of view of

the omniscient author (one who knows everything and seems to present narrative and comments objectively) has two major difficulties for the reader:

a) It is sometimes hard to accept that the writer can know everything – even the innermost thoughts and feelings of the characters;
b) the reader (or listener) has to 'suspend his disbelief', as Coleridge put it, for a time: he or she has to agree not to say, 'This is nonsense! How could the author know all this?'

The convention of the omniscient author is well established in the writing of fiction, however, and, provided the writer does not jar the audience into reactions where disbelief destroys the reader's involvement, it is one that is easily accepted – it is the point of view or stance most novelists have used in the past and continue to use today.
Let us now consider these points of view in detail.

The subjective approach

2.3

It is not easy to maintain a style of writing which uses a direct, first-person ('I', 'me', 'we', 'us') approach. Too often the writer's own personality comes through the writing in a way which is too intrusive, so that the reader begins to adopt, first, an irritated response and, later, an antagonistic response. Sometimes writers who use this style feel obliged to excuse themselves.

Consider, for example, this passage from Jonathan Swift's satirical proposal (published in 1729) to solve the Irish problem of overpopulation and poverty and the difficulty the rich gentry of London had in finding enough fresh meat to satisfy their tastes:

I shall now therefore humbly propose my own thoughts, which I hope will not be liable to the least objection.
I have been assured by a very knowing American of my acquaintance in London, that a young healthy child, well nursed, is at a year old a most delicious, nourishing, and wholesome food, whether stewed, roasted, baked, or boiled; and I make no doubt that it will equally serve in a fricassee or a ragout.
I do therefore humbly offer it to public consideration . . . that a hundred thousand may, at a year old, be offered in sale to the persons of quality and fortune through the kingdom, always advising the mother to let them suck plentifully in the last month, so as to render them plump and fat for a good table. A child will make two dishes at an entertainment for friends; and when the

family dines alone, the fore or hind quarter will make a reasonable dish, and seasoned with a little pepper or salt, will be very good boiled on the fourth day, especially in winter. . . .

I propose, in the sincerity of my heart, that I have not the least personal interest in endeavouring to promote this necessary work, *having no other motive than the public good of my country, by advancing our trade, providing for infants, relieving the poor, and giving some pleasure to the rich. I have no children by which I can propose to get a single penny; the youngest being nine years old, and my wife past child-bearing.*

Apart from the attack on the rich and their neglect of the poor inherent in this writing, Swift consciously sets the reader at his ease (and thereby leaves him vulnerable to the suggestion) by using a deliberately humble, disclaiming, personal style.

Another method used by writers to overcome the awkwardness of writing in the first person is to accept the challenge head-on and to use the style to advantage. For example, in his autobiography *Dear Me*, Peter Ustinov uses the personal style to great effect to amuse his reader:

Of the actual events surrounding my birth I remember very little. What I do know for certain is that, whereas I was born in London, I was in fact conceived in Leningrad. It stands to reason that I travelled a great deal during the more than nine months which separated my conception in the shadow of revolution and political slogan to my birth in the cold embrace of industrial smog and respectability.

2.4   *Let us consider, now, some typical writing situations in which the personal style of writing is used.*

Autobiography

2.5   Autobiography is an account of your own life – or part of it – with some thoughts or comments about it. This topic is frequently set in public examinations as the subject of a composition. For example:

a) A day I should like to forget.
b) The summer holiday I most enjoyed.
c) Memories of my earlier childhood.
d) My first visit to a slaughterhouse.
e) The day I started school.
f) The time I fell in love.
g) Living with mother and father.
h) Growing up in my family.

   i) The happiest (or saddest) moments in my life so far.
   j) The time I came to my senses.

In such exercises the writer's *point of view*, the *content* of the writing and its *context* are very clearly implicit – even if they are not explicitly stated. The one thing that is usually omitted is the 'audience', the person towards whom the writing is directed. Too often it is assumed that the audience is the teacher or some disembodied examiner. It is amazing just how frank and uninhibited the personal writing of some candidates can become when they are unburdening themselves of an experience or a thought; the revelations are sometimes frank and confessional in tone and substance.

The best writing of this kind attempts some of the following:

   a) to describe events (or a single event) clearly, with the details arranged in an order likely to produce a certain effect (e.g. satire, humour, nostalgia, tension, sadness, excitement, suspense);
   b) to evoke a mood;
   c) to present a comment, direct or indirect;
   d) to establish an interaction between events and writer which can lead to a sympathetic communication between the writer and the reader.

The secret of writing autobiographical accounts well lies in:

> selecting and ordering the material to be used;
> the use of contrasts, comparisons, and examples taken from personal observation and experience;
> choosing vocabulary which will evoke a mood;
> constructing sentences which, by their very shape, will enhance or clarify the point of the writing.

Consider, for example, the following passage from Laurie Lee's *Cider with Rosie*, where a single sentence at the end of the autobiography demonstrates this skill superbly:

> As for me – for me the grass grew longer, and more sorrowful, and the trees were surfaced like flesh, and girls were no longer to be treated lightly but were creatures of commanding sadness, and all journeys through the valley were now made alone, with passion in every bush, and the motions of wind and cloud and stars were suddenly for myself alone, and voices elected me of all men living and called me to deliver the world, and I groaned from solitude, blushed when I stumbled, loved strangers and bread and butter, and made long trips through the rain on my bicycle, stared wretchedly through lighted windows, grinned wryly to think how little I was known, and lived in a state of raging excitement.

Here the details come tumbling out, seemingly in wild profusion, but together they produce a rich tapestry of complex memories which evokes mood, comments on adolescent tensions, and touches off a sympathy between the writer and his unknown reader – unknown by name, but a boy or girl, man or woman with the same joys and agonies, thoughts, hopes and frustrations. There is ample evidence of the selection of material and its ordering, contrasts and comparisons, personal observation, evocative mood, and the technical control of pace within the sentence itself. (See how the word *and* is used by Laurie Lee to give this control.)

Diaries

2.6

Most diaries are written as a personal record of the events day by day in one's life. Uusually there is little thought of their being published and so the 'audience' frequently is the writer's own 'other person' or 'other image', a kind of personal double or *alter ego*, to whom the most intimate secrets and reflections can be revealed. Some diarists have even written in their own form of language to express this intimacy.

Take, for example, the famous diary of a Jewish girl, Anne Frank, who died in the concentration camp of Bergen-Belsen in March, 1945, three months before she would have been sixteen. She and her family went into hiding from the Gestapo in a tiny attic in Amsterdam in 1943. She kept a diary which was found in a pile of papers left by the Gestapo on 4 August 1944, when they raided the secret hide-out.

Anne Frank wrote intimately and sensitively about her thoughts and feelings in response to a terrifying situation. Her *point of view* was clear; the *content* of the diary was concerned with the events in the narrow, confined world of the attic; the *context* of the writing was one of fear, tension and adolescent uncertainty and tension. She created her own *audience* – the diary, which she addresses throughout as a person named 'Kitty':

> Friday, 7th January, 1944
>
> Dear Kitty,
>
> What a silly ass I am! I was quite forgetting that I have never told you the history of myself and all my boy friends. When I was quite small – I was even still at a kinder-

garten – I became attached to Karel Samson. He had lost his father, and he and his mother lived with an aunt. One of Karel's cousins, Robby, was a slender, good-looking dark boy, who aroused more admiration than the little, humorous podge Karel. But looks did not count with me and I was very fond of Karel for years...

Then Peter crossed my path, and in my childish way I really fell in love. He liked me very much, too, and we were inseparable for one whole summer...

I went to the Jewish Secondary School. Lots of boys in our class were keen on me – I thought it was fun, felt honoured, but was otherwise quite untouched. Then later on, Harry was mad about me, but, as I've already told you, I never fell in love again...

When Daddy kissed me this morning, I could have cried out: 'Oh, if only you were Peter!' I think of him all the time and I keep repeating to myself the whole day, 'Oh, Peter, darling, darling Peter...!' Oh Peter, Peter, how will I ever free myself of your image?...

Once, when we spoke about sex, Daddy told me that I couldn't possibly understand the longing yet; I always knew that I did understand it and now I understand it fully. Nothing is so beloved to me now as he, my Peter.

Yours,
Anne

The style of personal diaries, therefore, is marked by intimacy and self-revelation. The reader looks over the writer's shoulder and feels a little ashamed of his or her intrusion. The sentences tumble out one after the other in a flood of ideas and feelings. The writer experiments with words, expressions, and exclamations.

The most famous diary in the English language, perhaps, is that written by Samuel Pepys. It opens on 1 January 1660, when Pepys was poor and living in Westminster. His eyesight gradually failed him and he was obliged to give up his diary on 31 May 1669, but, nevertheless, it covered the exciting period in London of the Plague Year (1665) and the Great Fire (1666). It was written from Pepys's own *personal standpoint* in a system of shorthand which was not deciphered until 1825. The style is marked by the brief, often subject-less or verbless sentences; the *content* consists of the things Pepys did or observed, with his comments on them; the *context* is seventeenth-century London with all its upheavals and challenges to a sensitive, alert, civil servant; the writing is *directed* at himself as both writer and reader:

> *January 1st (Lord's Day) 1660.* This morning (we living lately in the garret) I rose, put on my suit with great skirts, having not lately worn any other clothes but them. Went to Mr Gunning's chapel at Exeter House, where he made a very good sermon. Dined at home in the garret, where my wife dressed the remains of a turkey, and in the doing of it she burned her hand.
>
> *July 10th, 1665.* To the office, in great trouble to see the Bill this week rise so high, to above 4,000 in all, and of them above 3,000 of the plague. After writing letters home to draw over anew my will, which I had bound myself by oath to dispatch by tomorrow night, the town growing so unhealthy that a man cannot depend upon living two days to an end. So having done something of it, I to bed.
>
> *September 2nd (Lord's Day), 1666.* Some of our maids sitting up late last night to get things ready against our feast today, Jane called us up about three in the morning to tell us of a great fire they saw in the City. So I rose and slipped on my night-gown and went to her window, and thought it to be on the back-side of Mark-Lane at the farthest; but being unused to such fires as followed, I thought it far enough off; and so went to bed again and to sleep.
>
> *31 May, 1669.* And thus ends all that I doubt I shall ever be able to do with my own eyes in the keeping of my Journal, I being not able to do it any longer, having done now so long as to undo my eyes every time that I take a pen in my hand . . . And so I betake myself to that course, which is almost as much as to see myself into my grave: for which, and all the discomforts that will accompany me being blind, the good God prepare me!
>
> S.P.

Personal responses to stimuli

2.7

The occasions in real life where one would want to set down in writing what one feels about a painting, a piece of music, or a poem are rare;

more often such responses are likely to be given in conversation, where two friends meet and discuss the latest science-fiction book they have read, the latest album they have bought and listened to, or the latest visit they have made, say, to a theatre, a cinema, a museum, or an art-gallery. Nevertheless, exercises in school or college often ask for personal written responses to such stimuli.

The difficulty with such exercises lies in the fact, however, that the 'audience' or reader is rarely specified. The writer, therefore, has to fall back on choosing consciously or subconsciously, before he or she begins to write, for whom the writing is intended. Usually the 'audience' remains vague and undefined in examination exercises but the best personal writing emerges when it is *directed* towards a reader.

Consider, for example, what responses would be stimulated in a writer who has just received one of the following notes and feels the need to reply. How would he or she react? What kind of writing could be used in a response? What should be said? (Decide on the 'context' before you decide.)

a)

> Dear Paul,
>   Sorry about last night, but you had to know. For some time now it's all been different between us. We just don't think alike any more. I suppose I could have told you differently and chosen a better time, but I feel much happier now I've said it and it's all over.
>
>   Please don't blame me too much. I did love you and still like you quite a bit.
>   Thanks for all the happy moments.
>   See you around,   Sue

b)

Dear Mrs Hanson,

I am writing to tell you that your dog has done it again! I really did think that last time I made it perfectly clear! I will not tolerate his continual barking at three o'clock in the morning!

My husband has to be up for work at five o'clock and needs his rest. How can he sleep if your animal is yapping all night long?

Unless you do something – straightaway – I'll telephone the police next time and have him put down.

Yours angrily,
Mrs Hanratty (at number 56)

c)

Keep Burglars Out

Free home surveys.
Professional, friendly, helpful advice.

**Alarms. Sirens. Immobilisers.
Grilles. Deadlocks.**

Mobile fitting service.
Trade or domestic.

Why not drop us a line?
Write to ALARMABURGLA, Rosedale Avenue, Twickenham TW19 7XZ.

2.8   Where the audience remains unspecified in a personal writing exercise, however, it is usually helpful to establish such an audience for yourself before beginning your work. Decide how you are going to direct your writing; there are a number of ways in which this can be done, including the following suggestions:

a) Decide to write in an autobiographical or diary form. (See above, pp. 18–22.)

b) Address yourself by writing meditatively, thoughtfully, intro-
   spectively – almost as if you are thinking aloud (e.g. in response
   to the picture of the bombed library (see p. 34)):

I remember the library. It's odd now I never managed to go inside
before – although I always wanted to.

  Go on! Open the door – that's all you've got to do! But what if
Old Grumpy's there? The one with the peaked cap! He'll only
scream and shout at me: 'Clear off! This is a library, not a
playground!'

  Now anyone can go in. Even me, I suppose. Here we go then.
Mind the débris. It's a shame that all these leather-bound books
are covered in dust. Oops! I nearly came a cropper that time;
didn't see that ladder.

  Where shall I start? Mustn't disturb the other readers. They've
all kept their hats on. Must be going to rain or something! . . .

c) Invent an audience by writing *a letter* addressed to a specific
   person (a relative, a friend, a colleague) or *an article* (for a
   newspaper, a magazine, a pamphlet, a handbook) or some
   imaginary or imagined person.

   e.g. In 1952 the BBC asked a number of distinguished men to
   write letters to people who would be alive in 2052. The broad-
   casts were called *Letters to Posterity*. A scientist, Dr Jacob
   Bronowski, wrote to his great-grandchildren.

My Dear Great-Grandchildren,

          You will not remember
me. I am the scientist in the
family album; the one near the
front, with the glasses and the
earnest look. I am by training
and, I hope, by taste a geometer.
That means I do not speculate
about things, but about the
relations between things: their
pattern or arrangement – the angles
in a triangle, the shape of a crystal,
or an extra dimension . . . .
     I give you this picture of

myself because I cannot picture you at all. I cannot picture where you live, what you do, how you dress or travel. For all I know, you may have pumped a lake into the Sahara and be growing seaweed there to make synthetic fish-cakes. Or you may be shuttling round the earth on a space platform, armoured in some metal I do not even know, to keep off the cosmic rays. Whatever I might guess about your physical life a hundred years from now is sure to be wrong. Yet I have no doubt at all that I know how you will think . . . .

d) Construct a narrative or a dramatic piece of dialogue in which you can play a role as one of the major characters, ready to reveal your own thoughts and motives as well as describe your own actions.

e.g. Edward Blishen is a well-known writer and broadcaster who has taught in a number of schools. He wrote about his experiences as a schoolmaster:

'And so this morning I'd like you to write something that could be called "My Autobiography".'

The displeasure was general.

'I haven't done anything, sir,' said Matthews.

'My life's just dull,' said Gilligan. 'My mum wouldn't let me do anything interesting anyway.'

Blaire hid a snigger.

'Adventures don't have to be very big to be adventures,' I said.

'Tonsillitis,' said Gilligan cryptically.

I knew I had on my side their natural disposition, once they had started, to become absorbed in any composition. If the worst came to the worst, I could get something out of them about the life cycle of a fungus. 'Now get on,' I called above the shuffle of discontent. They became silent.

Within five minutes the board was covered with the names of the chief infantile diseases. . . .

Objective accounts of experiences

2.9

The skill involved in describing an event or process experienced personally by the writer is one often needed in the writing of a personal report. The subject *content* is normally precisely determined, the *context* in which the report is being written is established (reports are usually written for a purpose to describe accurately an event or a process for some other person in authority, or a committee, or a client), and the *audience* is explicitly or implicitly clear.

The basic problem here for writers is one of organisation of the facts to be used. Very often the writer is still working out the ideas as he or she is writing but, added to the difficulty of working out the ideas and their significance, is the additional problem of directing the material towards a reader.

Consider for example these three descriptions of a road accident:

a) At 3.43 an articulated Foden lorry approached the pedestrian crossing at Stickleback Lane. The crossing lights changed, the driver braked, the lorry skidded on the wet road and jack-knifed across the crossing itself. Michael Roberts, aged 14, was struck by the lorry and killed instantly.

b) At 3.43 I saw a lorry with a trailer on it coming to the pedestrian crossing at the top of Stickleback Lane. Just as it got to the crossing, the lights changed and the driver jammed on his brakes. The wheels skidded and the back of the lorry swung round towards us and hit Michael. I think he is dead.

c) I saw it all, Mum. We'd just come out of school – about a quarter to four it was. When we got to the crossing, you know, the one in Stickleback Lane, the lights changed and a big lorry skidded on the wet road. It came straight at us – the back did – because it sort of came round. It missed me but knocked Michael over. It was awful! He looked as if he was dead to me.

The first (a) is an objective account setting out the bare facts; the second (b) is a statement made by a witness to a policeman; the third (c) is a description of what happened given later by the same witness to her mother. One account (a) is written; (b) is a spoken statement, later rendered into formal written English; (c) is a spoken statement set down just as it was given orally. Reports are usually made in styles nearer to that of (a) or of (b). *Can you distinguish some of the differences in the language of the three examples?*

2.10   Reports or accounts of experiments in scientific subjects such as Chemistry, Physics, or Biology demand a recognised style where the writing is really intended as a personal record for the student himself or herself rather than a 'personalised' objective report directed at the teacher. In such accounts the viewpoint may be personal, but the facts need to be objectively selected and considered; to keep these two points distinct in the writing calls for a degree of skill in judging the levels ('registers') on which the English Language operates.

Consider, for example, the following two accounts of an experiment to demonstrate Archimedes' principle (which explains amongst other things why huge, steel ships float on water but blocks of solid iron sink). In the first, the experiment is described objectively, for a student reading a textbook; in the second, the same experiment is reported *personally* in the first person, by a writer for his or her own use.

What differences can you see in the way the language is used in the two reports?

a) Fluid pressure is responsible for the upthrust or buoyancy of a body immersed in a fluid. For a body to float on a liquid, e.g. a piece of wood or cork on water, it must be buoyed up by an upward thrust.

The problem was first investigated by Archimedes who explained how to calculate the size of the upthrust:

'When a body is totally or partially immersed in a fluid, it experiences an upthrust equal to the weight of the mass of fluid displaced.' (The term 'fluid' means gas or liquid.)

To demonstrate this experimentally, lower a stone into a displacement can. The water which the stone displaces overflows and, when weighed, is found to have a weight equal to the upthrust.

b) I filled a large eureka can with water and let any excess water run out through the side-spout. When the spout had finished dripping I put a beaker under it.

Then I hung a stone on a spring-balance and lowered the stone into the water. Surprise of surprises, as the stone went further into the water it seemed to lose weight on the spring-balance's scale and water from the can was pushed out into the beaker. Every time it lost ten grams of weight on the scale, I experimented and found it had pushed out ten grams of water into the beaker.

When I used a jam jar, instead of a stone, to repeat the experiment by the time the jam jar seemed to have lost all its weight on the scale, it had pushed out of the can enough water to equal its original weight in the air – and the jar was floating!

It seems to me, then, that if an object can displace its own weight of water before it becomes totally submerged, it ought to float. Come to think of it, that's why the *Britannia* doesn't go straight to the bottom with the Queen and everyone else on it.

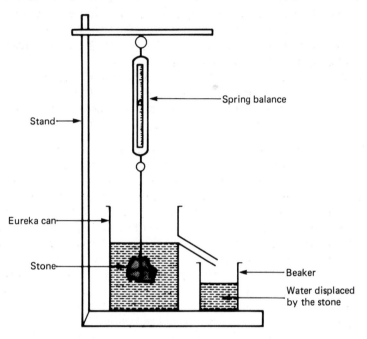

Stand

Spring balance

Eureka can

Stone

Beaker

Water displaced by the stone

Personal arguments and discussion

It often happens that one is called upon to present a case for or against a personally held (or rejected) belief.

The following topics were set in a recent public examination:

a) Argue the case for *either* believing in *or* not believing in one of the following:

    i)   life on other planets;
    ii) monsters such as the Loch Ness Monster or the Abdominable Snowman;
    iii) faith-healing;
    iv) reincarnation;
    v)   popular superstitions.

b) Make a case for the compulsory study of one of the following in school or college:

2.11

Religious Studies; Politics; English Literature; Art; Computer Studies; Home Economics.

The rubrics to the questions establish quite clearly the point of view required of the candidate before writing: that of a supporter or that of an opposer. Of course, the writing offered might have been *personally* presented or *impersonally* presented. Very often the best writing on such topics arises when personal beliefs are strongly presented with personal examples from a personal point of view.

Consider the following extracts from Winston Churchill's essay on *Painting as a Pastime*; they express his personal delight in painting and advocate it as a hobby for older people and as a way of relieving anxiety and taking away pressure in life:

I do not submit these sketches to the public gaze because I am under any illusion about their merit. They are the productions of a week-end and holiday amateur who during the last few years has found a new pleasure, and who wishes to tell others of his luck. To have reached the age of forty without ever handling a brush or fiddling with a pencil, to have regarded with mature eye the painting of pictures of any kind as a mystery, to have stood agape before the chalk of a pavement artist, and then suddenly to find oneself plunged in the middle of a new and intense form of interest and action with paints and palettes and canvases, and not to be discouraged by results, is an astonishing and enriching experience. I hope it may be shared by others. . . .

Just to paint is great fun. The colours are lovely to look at and delicious to squeeze out . . . Try it if you have not done so, before you die . . .

There really is no time for the deliberate approach.

Two years of drawing lessons, three years of copying wood-cuts, five years of plaster casts – these are for the young . . . We must not be too ambitious. We cannot aspire to masterpieces. We may content ourselves with a joy-ride in a paintbox. I shall now relate my personal experience. When I left the Admiralty at the end of May, 1915, I still remained a member of the Cabinet and of the War Council. The change from the intensive executive activities of each day's work at the Admiralty to the narrowly-measured duties of a counsellor left me gasping. Like a sea-beast fished up from the depths, or a diver too suddenly hoisted, my veins threatened to burst from the fall in pressure. I had great anxiety and no means of relieving it; I had vehement convictions and small power to give effect to them. I had long hours of utterly unwonted leisure in which to contemplate the unfolding of the War. And then it was that the Muse of Painting came to my rescue.

Churchill's point of view is personal yet the argument is explicit. He writes from his own personal experience in order to make his case for taking up painting – even late in life.

Personal arguments need not be quite so explicit, however. The gin-trap was once widely used by poachers and others to snare wild creatures in the English countryside. It was particularly vicious and left many wild creatures to die in long-drawn-out agony. Following a long campaign by writers, journalists, naturalists and others it was finally made illegal. The following extract comes from an article in *The Evening News* written by Oswald Barron ('The Londoner'); its point of view is clear – that of an opponent of the cruel gin-trap – and the writing is intensely personal. It argues the case against cruelty to wild-life very powerfully – the more so, since the argument is deeply implicit in the writing.:

> It was the quiet hour before the grass darkens; the world seemed all at peace in that corner until I saw the earth stir under the hedge.
>
> There was the broad porch of an old rabbit-burrow and the earth stirred in it. I crept near to see what was alive in that place. I knew very soon, so soon as I heard a rusty chain chink at its staple. It was the chain of a gin.
>
> I drew at the chain and brought out the gin. Its jaws had snapped upon the legs and shoulder of a stoat. The valiant little beast was striving hard for its life; its red back writhed and strained. For a moment its bright eyes looked at me; you would have said that for a moment it wondered, despairing, if I might be deliverance from the iron teeth that mangled it. Then it strained and dragged again upon the wound, stubbornly, without a cry. . . .
>
> You will teach me nothing about the stoat and his way of life. I know very well that this little beast is bloody and merciless beyond all other beasts. He is the assassin of the hedgerows. I have seen him with his sharp teeth behind the head of a scream-ing rabbit. Therefore he may not plead for mercy; indeed, he never asks it; he will die silently when the end comes; this one never cried aloud in the agony of the trap. Yet it went to my heart to kill that beautiful fierce thing; I would that the foul duty had been laid on another.
>
> Nevertheless I killed; it sickened me that I should have to kill a beast that was at my mercy. But I killed the stoat, and I knew that I could not do otherwise.

What features of this kind of writing give it its immediate and telling impact? Consider especially the ways in which the writer indicates his own inner reactions and feelings.

Exercises

1 Write a personal letter to the Prime Minister setting out your views about some action which s/he and the government have taken. (It may be an action with which you agree or disagree strongly. If you wish, you might, after reading 2.3 above, attempt a satirical letter.)

2 Write a chapter suitable for your own autobiography, which you hope a plublisher will want to print, on one of the composition topics set out in 2.5 above, pp. 18–20. (This section of Chapter 2 gives you some help about approaches to include and ideas to use.)

3 Write an account (for your own personal pleasure in setting it down) of the most exciting thing that ever happened to you. Restrict yourself to 200 words but make every single word contribute to the sense of excitement. (You should draft and re-draft this work until you are satisfied that it conveys the thrill as strongly as you can.)

4 Write a 200-word account of what you did yesterday which would be suitable for inclusion in a personal diary if you were to keep one. (You will find it helpful to re-read 2.6 above, pp. 20–22, before you begin to plan your writing.)

5 Write a narrative, a descriptive, or a discussion essay (about 450 words) on a topic suggested by one of the pictures on pp. 34–5. (Your writing should be based on a central feature of the picture and not on a minor, peripheral detail.)

6   Now first, as I shut the door,
      I was alone
      In the new house; and the wind
      Began to moan.
                (E. Thomas, 1878–1917)

   Give your own reactions, in the form of a letter to a friend, to a house you have just entered for the very first time or come to live in.

7 Set out your own views, for inclusion in a magazine aimed at the teenage market, of a film or new record album or an exhibition you have recently enjoyed. (Make sure that your enjoyment shows in the writing.)

8 Imagine that you have been to a party which was 'gatecrashed' by some young people who were totally unknown to you. The party

ended with a smashed house, two people taken to hospital with severe physical injuries, and an investigation by the police.

Write three accounts of the end of the party as follows:

a) an objective report of the bare facts (in about 100 words);
b) a statement, later written down, made by you to the police (in about 150 words); and
c) a description given by you to your parents once you managed to arrive home. (This will have been an *oral* account and will necessarily be colloquial in its tone; restrict yourself to not more than 250 words.)

9 Write an account of *either* a famous battle *or* a famous discovery as you would present it as part of your History course work. (You may, if you wish, refer briefly to its significance and its consequences.)

10 Argue the case for *either* believing in *or* not believing in one of the following to someone who holds the opposite view:

a) the fundamental goodness of mankind;
b) life after death;
c) the equality of all men and women;
d) anarchy;
e) the coming of a future golden age on earth.

11 Make a case out in a letter to your member of parliament for *one* of the following:

a) lowering the school-leaving age to fourteen;
b) abolishing private education;
c) paying everyone the same wage;
d) abolishing unilateral defence systems;
c) appointing you as his or her personal adviser.

12 Using the Principle of Archimedes (see 2.10 above, pp. 28–9), try to give an explanation to an intelligent ten-year-old who has asked you in the course of a conversation on the top deck of a bus passing the docks, why huge, steel ships don't sink. Write down what you would say. (Make a diagram, too, if you wish.)

13 Give a personal account of your hobby in an attempt to persuade the reader that it has important features to help him or her lead a happier life, too.

'There is no drama without conflict', and very often an effective way of presenting narrative, description, or discussion to an audience or to a reader is to put two or more people into a context where they can react to each other and press each other to develop ideas, stances, or moods. *On the stage* this is done by presenting characters within a play; *in written prose or verse* it is done by passages of dialogue in direct or reported speech; *in everyday colloquial situations* it is done by conversation accompanied by such features as gesture, expression, intonation, stress, repetition and hesitation.

Formal stage drama

3.1

In Shakespeare's play *Hamlet*, the main character, the Prince of Denmark, often communes with himself in **soliloquies** (talking to himself when no-one else is present); he establishes his own point of view, debates his problem, and gives his analysis of the possible solutions. The dialogue is between himself and aspects of his own character. In the following famous passage he debates with himself whether it is better to continue living with all the pains and troubles of life or to die. The two sides of the argument are put in an intensely personal manner:

> To be, or not to be, that is the question:
> Whether 'tis nobler in the mind to suffer
> The slings and arrows of outrageous fortune,
> Or to take arms against a sea of troubles
> And by opposing end them. To die – to sleep
> No more; and by a sleep to say we end
> The heart-ache and the thousand natural shocks
> That flesh is heir to: 'tis a consummation
> Devoutly to be wish'd. To die, to sleep;
> To sleep, perchance to dream – ay, there's the rub:
> For in that sleep of death what dreams may come,
> When we have shuffled off this mortal coil,

Must give us pause – there's the respect
That makes calamity of so long life.
For who would bear the whips and scorns of time,
Th'oppressor's wrong, the proud man's contumely,
The pangs of dispriz'd love, the law's delay,
The insolence of office, and the spurns
That patient merit of th'unworthy takes,
When he himself might his quietus make
With a bare bodkin? Who would fardels bear,
To grunt and sweat under a weary life,
But that the dread of something after death,
The undiscover'd country, from whose bourn
No traveller returns, puzzles the will,
And makes us rather bear those ills we have
Than fly to others that we know not of?
Thus conscience does make cowards of us all,
And thus the native hue of resolution
Is sicklied o'er with the pale cast of thought,
And enterprises of great pitch and moment
With this regard their currents turn awry
And lose the name of action.

Usually, however, the 'conflict' is presented in the form of an exchange of **dialogue** between the characters. In Bernard Shaw's play *Androcles and the Lion* (first produced in London in 1913), the Christian arguments for pacifism and against pacifism are presented in this humorous extract:

3.2

CAESAR:	The hour has come, Ferrovius. I shall go into my box and see you killed, since you scorn the Pretorian Guard.
LAVINIA	*(to Ferrovius)*: Farewell.
THE EDITOR:*	Steady there. You Christians have got to fight. Here! arm yourselves.
FERROVIUS	*(picking up a sword)*: I'll die sword in hand to show people that I could fight if it were my Master's will, and that I could kill the man who kills me if I chose.
THE EDITOR:	Put on that armour.
FERROVIUS:	No armour.
THE EDITOR	*(bullying him)*: Do what you're told. Put on that armour.
FERROVIUS	*(gripping the sword and looking dangerous)*: I said, no armour.
THE EDITOR:	And what am I to say when I am accused of sending a naked man in to fight my men in armour?

FERROVIUS:	Say your prayers, brother, and have no fear of the princes of this world.
THE EDITOR:	You obstinate fool.
ANDROCLES	*(to Ferrovius)*: Farewell, brother, till we meet in the sweet by-and-by.
THE EDITOR	*(to Androcles)*: You are going too. Take a sword there, and put on any armour you can find to fit you.
ANDROCLES:	No, really: I can't fight: I never could: I can't bring myself to dislike anyone enough. I'm to be thrown to the lions with the lady. (* The man responsible for the Gladiators)

Notice, particularly here, the way in which Shaw differentiates his characters and gives all five of them very clear points of view from which to argue. The humour in the passage springs very largely from the clashes in those viewpoints.

3.3   Some examinations give candidates an opportunity to write in dramatic form, if they wish. It is not easy to develop a situation dramatically, but many who have some practice in producing this form of writing are highly successful in a) establishing characters, b) exploring a situation and its conflict(s), and c) developing the plot with the help of one or more crises. These three elements are vital to the success of dramatic writing, but at its heart, too, lies the need to establish clearly differentiated points of view for the characters.

Consider carefully how you might develop the dramatic situation presented in the following:

A living-room in a large suburban house. The family are waiting for Mr Hillcroft to arrive home from work before they begin their evening meal. He is obviously very late and his wife looks anxiously at the clock above the fireplace. Jill is fifteen and curled up in an armchair reading; Graham, her brother, is twelve and is finishing a model of a spacecraft. A key turns the lock in the front door and Mr Hillcroft comes puffing into the room, showering the carpet with drops from his raincoat.

MRS HILLCROFT	*(angry)*: You *are* late. Wherever have you been?
MR HILLCROFT:	Haven't you seen the news? The crowds, Nell! You should have seen them! They were carrying a coffin!
GRAHAM	*(interested)*: A coffin?
JILL	*(looking up and demolishing her brother)*: Not a real one, stupid! They were protesting about the Bomb!
MR HILLCROFT:	Protests or not, they stopped me from getting home.

JILL   (*earnestly now*): It's a good job someone
                protests; that coffin could be ours soon.
*The door opens and standing in the doorway is an
eighteen-year-old boy with cropped hair, dirty jeans, and heavy
boots.*
THE BOY   (*gruffly*): Sorry. I saw the door open and so I
                came in.

Written prose or verse

3.4

Here a distinction is made between direct speech and reported or
indirect speech. In both forms of writing, however, the points of view
of the speakers (and of the writer himself or herself) must be clear either
explicitly or implicitly.
Direct speech quotes the actual words used by a character.
    e.g. He said, 'I think I am dying.'
The words actually used are placed in inverted commas. The words
introducing those quoted may precede or follow:
    e.g. 'I think I am dying,' he said.
Reported (or indirect) speech reports the words said without actually
using the words originally spoken:
    e.g. He said (that) he thought he was dying.
Inverted commas are not needed with reported speech.

3.5

In changing direct speech into reported speech, a number of changes
have to be made:

a) Pronouns used have to change from the first and second persons
    to the third:

Subject	Object
I > he, she	*me* > him, her
we > they	*us* > them
you > he, she, they	*you* > them

    e.g.

    He said, '*I* think *I* am dying.' (Direct)
    He said *he* thought *he* was dying. (Reported)
    He ordered the girl, 'Pay *me* for the book.' (Direct)
    He ordered the girl to pay *him* for the book. (Reported)
    She said, '*We* shall obey.' (Direct)
    She said *they* would obey. (Reported)
    She said, 'The boy saw *us* getting on the bus.' (Direct)
    She said the boy had seen *them* getting on the bus.
        (Reported)

He complained, '*You* never kept *your* bargain.' (Direct)
He complained that *he* (she, they) had never kept his (*her, their*) bargain. (Reported)

b) Verbs will all be used in the third person (singular or plural) in reported speech or in the infinitive form in reported commands; the tenses also have to change into a more distant past tense: e.g.

He said, 'I *think* I *am* dying.' (Direct)
He said he *thought* he *was* dying. (Reported)
He commanded, '*Come* here.' (Direct Command)
He commanded (him, her, them) *to come* here (*or to go* there). (Reported)

c) Other changes may be necessary but the sense will determine whether such changes need to be made. Always think carefully about meanings when using reported speech. What differences in meaning can you establish between the following examples of reported speech?

He said he liked *this* girl.
He said he liked *that* girl.
She said he could come *tomorrow*.
She said she could come *the next day*.
They said they could be *here* tomorrow.
They said they could be *there* tomorrow.
He said they had arrived two days *ago*.
He said they had arrived two days *before*.

3.6   Dialogue, in either direct or reported speech, plays an important role in written English. Often novelists (or writers of other forms of fiction) introduce passages of dialogue to break up, or give a fresh immediacy to, a passage of narrative. Such switches can highlight a change of perspective or a change of point of view in a most dramatic manner.

3.7   In a delightful short story, *The Inexperienced Ghost* (first published in 1902), H. G. Wells narrates the first time a ghost goes out haunting, clad in the traditional white sheet, in a long corridor in a gentleman's club. The narrative changes its point of view from narrative to club member to ghost with astonishing rapidity, through dialogue to description and back to dialogue again – with great humorous effect. But the characters are clearly differentiated. (Notice, too, that the narrator is directly addressing an audience, some other members of the club, in describing his adventure with the ghost.)

I came upon him, you know, in the long passage. His back was towards me, and I saw him first. Right off I knew him for a ghost. He was transparent, and whitish; clean through his chest I could see the glimmer of the little window at the end . . .

I suppose I wasn't on the landing a moment before he found out I was there. So for an instant we stood – he looking over his shoulder at me – and regarded one another. Then he seemed to remember his high calling. He turned round, drew himself up; projected his face, raised his arms, spread his hands in approved ghost fashion – came towards me. As he did so his little jaw dropped, and he emitted a faint, drawn-out 'Boo!'

'Boo!' I said. 'Nonsense. You don't belong to this place. What are you doing here? Are you a member?'

'No,' he said, in answer to the persistent interrogation of my eye; 'I'm not a member – I'm a ghost.'

'Well, that doesn't give you the run of the Mermaid Club. Is there anyone you want to see, or anything of that sort?'

'I'm haunting,' he said.

'You haven't any business to,' I said in a quiet voice.

'I'm a ghost,' he said, as if in defence.

'That may be, but you haven't any business to haunt here. This is a respectable private club. You haven't any claim on this place, have you? Weren't murdered here, or anything of that sort?'

'None, sir, but I thought as it was old and oak-panelled –'

'That's no excuse.' I regarded him firmly. 'If I were you I wouldn't wait for cock-crow – I'd vanish right away.'

He looked embarrassed. 'The fact is, sir, –' he began.

'I'd vanish,' I said, driving it home.

'The fact is, sir, that – somehow – I can't!'

'You *can't*?'

'No, sir. There's something I've forgotten. I've tried to do it several times and it doesn't come off.'

Sometimes the dialogue can be reported in the third person just as effectively, without diminishing the effect of the point of view of the writer, the narrator, or the major characters.

In the following extract describing part of the trial at Nuremberg in 1945–6 of Hermann Göring, Reich Marshal and Commander-in-Chief of the Luftwaffe during the Second World War, the attitude and character of Göring, the stance of his defence counsel, the opinions of the narrator, who was a British officer, and the points of view of all three clearly emerge from the reported accounts of what was said:

3.8

But Göring was no buffoon, no mere 'fat man' of the cartoonists. By utterance and influence he showed himself to be one of the shrewdest men in the dock. With ringing defiance he was prepared to justify the Nazi revolution and everything that properly belonged to the affairs of a sovereign state. For him anything redounding to the greatness of the Reich was permissible, though no man had done more to avoid war, as he strove to prove by producing evidence – it turned out to be an ugly boomerang – of the aircraft that flew secretly between Berlin and London in the last days of peace carrying his envoy to the British Cabinet.

War for Göring came from an inexplicable constellation of the Powers, as war always did. Germany had never wanted it. And from this as the defence proceeded you could almost imagine that Germany had been the victim of a vast European plot to fall upon her. 'Had Poland shown a spark of goodwill,' argued Göring's counsel, 'there would have been no war,' a remark that earns its place in an anthology of cynicism. If Britain had not intervened with her guarantee, the reasoning ran, the Poles would never have been so stupid as to fight.

Above all, declared Göring, the German people were free of guilt. They could not call the führers to account and at the same time punish the people who, without knowledge of the grave crimes disclosed today, had courageously endured the struggle for existence, the struggle to the death.

Dialogue in verse

3.9 The use of dialogue in verse to establish the point of view of speakers, their relationship with each other, a context and an atmosphere and to advance a narrative is very well achieved in some ballads. Consider, for example the two main characters, their relationship, and their situation in the following poem written by W. H. Auden which proceeds entirely by dialogue as the tension mounts:

O what is that Sound which so thrills the ear
   Down in the valley drumming, drumming?
Only the scarlet soldiers, dear,
   The soldiers coming.
O what is that light I see flashing so clear
   Over the distance brightly, brightly?
Only the sun on their weapons, dear,
   As they step lightly.
O what are they doing with all that gear;
   What are they doing this morning, this morning?
Only the usual manoeuvres, dear,
   Or perhaps a warning.
O why have they left the road down there;
   Why are they suddenly wheeling, wheeling?
Perhaps a change in the orders, dear;
   Why are you kneeling?

O haven't they stopped for the doctor's care;
　Haven't they reined their horses, their horses?
Why, they are none of them wounded, dear,
　None of these forces.
O is it the parson they want with white hair;
　Is it the parson, is it, is it?
No, they are passing his gateway, dear,
　Without a visit.
O it must be the farmer who lives so near;
　It must be the farmer so cunning, so cunning?
They have passed the farm already, dear,
　And now they are running.
O where are you going? stay with me here!
　Were the vows you swore so deceiving, deceiving?
No, I promised to love you, dear,
　But I must be leaving.
O it's broken the lock and splintered the door,
　O it's the gate where they're turning, turning;
Their boots are heavy on the floor
　And their eyes are burning.

Everyday colloquial situations

When two or more people take part in a conversation the relationship
between the speakers as well as the topic and the context will help to
determine the kind of English that is used. The points of view themselves may even change as the relationship alters.

　Take, for example, a situation where a boy and a girl meet for the first
time at a party. Each is attracted to the other and would like to develop
a friendship, but the opening conversation may well be awkward,
edgy, hesitant as each jockeys for position. When a topic of real
interest to them both arises the language will become more easy and
relaxed; the points of view become more readily defined.

3.10

CLIVE:　Hello. You here on your own?
JULIE:　Yes. How about you?
CLIVE:　Yes.
JULIE:　Do you know anybody?
CLIVE:　Only Sue – she's the one giving the party.
JULIE:　Oh.
CLIVE:　Who asked you?
JULIE:　Sue. We went to school together.
CLIVE:　So you know Sue, too, do you? She's great.

JULIE: Yes. We were in the same year.
CLIVE: What do you do?
JULIE: Do?
CLIVE: You know, for work?
JULIE: I'm at college.
CLIVE: Which one?
JULIE: The tech.
CLIVE: No! I go there, too! I've never seen you.
JULIE: I've never seen *you*! What are you studying?
CLIVE: French and German. You?
JULIE: Engineering.
CLIVE: That's great! I'm studying languages and you, a girl, studying Engineering!
JULIE: What's wrong with that? You're not a male chauvinist pig, are you?
CLIVE: As a matter of fact I am. After all, 'Engineering'! What do you see in it?
JULIE: It's all right once you get into it. The beginning of the course is the worst. We had to . . .

3.11   In *The Times* recently Miles Kington produced a delightful conversation between a sales manager of a firm selling second-hand grand pianos and a potential customer; the scene is modelled on a more typical sales situation – that of selling a second-hand car. Notice the flexible way the points of view of the two men change as the conversation develops and the effect the change has on the language they use. A key question to answer is: How does the relationship differ at the end of the discussion from what it was at the beginning?

You'll need a starting Handel, squire.

Miles Kington

'You can get an upright piano for just over £1,000. And that's not bad when you think you are buying something with 5,000 parts' – Mary Baxter, Piano Publicity Association.

The scene is the forecourt of Sid's new and used pianos, a large repair and tuning depot just off the North Circular Road. The manager, who is wearing a sheepskin jacket and a badge reading 'Schubert's Unfinished and I'm Not Feeling Too Great Myself', is standing there wiping his dusty hands. A customer comes up to him, pushing an old upright.

Customer: Sid?

Manager: He's not here.

Customer: Do you know where he is?

Manager: No idea. He died in 1947. We kept the name for tax purposes.

Customer: Ah. Well, if you're in charge, I wonder if you could have a look at my piano. I'm having a bit of trouble with it at speed.

Manager: Sure. Just park it over by that yellow Bechstein and we'll give it the once over at the weekend.

Customer: I'd be grateful if you could have a look now. I need it this evening.

Manager: All right, squire. *(He opens the top and hits the keys once or twice.)* Blimey, I'm not surprised you've been having trouble. When did you last clean the return mechanism?

Customer: Well, I . . .

Manager: Got to keep the return mechanism clean. When it gets dirty, it starts to stick and then you can't get those repeated notes, know what I mean?

Customer: So it's the return mechanism needs cleaning, is it? That's a relief.

Manager: And these hammers are worn. Oh dear, oh dear, oh dear. Worn? They're more like cotton wool on a stick than hammers. And look at these strings. Oh deary, deary me.

Customer: Is it bad then?

Manager: Bad? I'm not saying it's bad. I'm just saying that considering it's an old Carl Schumann piano, made in Dresden 70 years ago, you're lucky it's still going at all. What do you use it for?

Customer: Beethoven, mostly. Though I quite often relax with some boogie-woogie.

Manager: Well, there you are then. That stuff really punishes a piano.

Customer: It's very quiet boogie-woogie.

Manager: Boogie-woogie? I'm talking about your actual Beethoven. He's murder on a little old upright like this. Quite honestly, squire, it's hardly worth mending this lot. Know what I'd do? I'd put in a factory reconditioned frame and new set of strings and hammers. I could do it for £600, sir.

Customer: £600!

Manager: We'd reline the pedals and put in a new sustainer as well, of course. All in the price. And top it up with new varnish.

Customer: It's almost like buying a new piano . . .

Manager: Now you're talking! By complete coincidence, I have here a wonderful upright, only one previous owner, a little lady who stuck to Mozart all her life and never went faster than moderato, straight up! Only just gone on sale. Bound to be snapped up by the weekend.

Customer: But I only came in to get a quick overhaul, not a whole new piano.

Manager: Suit yourself, mate. You want to push on with the old one, that's your privilege.

Customer: Well . . . how much are you asking?

Manager: £1,100.

Customer: *£1,100,* for this old thing?

Manager: It's got a beautiful response, this machine. Nice tuning, lovely action. Tell you what, I'll make it £1,050. Couldn't bring it lower without bankrupting myself.

At this point the assistant manager comes over and joins the discussion. He remonstrates angrily when he finds that the manager is prepared to let it go for just over £1,000. The manager says he's sorry, but he's already given his word to this gentleman. The assistant manager storms off furiously. Later that evening he and the manager dine out on salmon and champagne to celebrate the sale of a piano that cost them only £170.

What do you think is the point of view from which Miles Kington wrote this piece? Is it the kind of situation, given a change or two here and there, in which you have ever found yourself? How does the language track the developing relationship between the speakers?

Exercises

1 After the murder of Julius Caesar in Shakespeare's play, the two main conspirators fall out. There is a violent argument between Brutus and Cassius. Imagine that you were a soldier on guard in the tent where the argument took place; when you come off duty report in detail to a fellow soldier in the Roman guard-room what the two men said.

CASSIUS: That you have wrong'd me doth appear in this.
You have condemned and noted Lucius Pella
For taking bribes here of the Sardians;
Wherein my letters, praying on his side,
Because I knew the man, were slighted off.

BRUTUS: You wrong'd yourself to write in such a case . . .
Let me tell you, Cassius, you yourself
Are much condemned to have an itching palm;
To sell and mart your offices for gold
To undeservers.

CASSIUS: I an itching palm! You know that you are Brutus that speaks this,
Or, by the gods, this speech were
else your last . . .
I'll not endure it: you forget yourself
To hedge me in. I am a soldier, I,
Older in practice, abler than yourself
To make conditions.

BRUTUS: Go to; you are not Cassius.

CASSIUS: I am.

BRUTUS: I say you are not.

CASSIUS: Urge me no more, I shall forget myself;
Have mind upon your health; tempt me no
further . . .

BRUTUS: You say you are a better soldier:
Let it appear so; make your vaunting true,
And it shall please me well . . .

CASSIUS: You wrong me every way; you wrong me,

Brutus; I said an elder soldier, not a better:
Did I say, 'better'?

BRUTUS:	If you did, I care not.
CASSIUS:	When Caesar liv'd, he durst not thus have moved me.
BRUTUS:	Peace, peace? You durst not so have tempted him.
CASSIUS:	I durst not!
BRUTUS:	No.
CASSIUS:	What! durst not tempt him!
BRUTUS:	For your life you durst not.
CASSIUS:	Do not presume too much upon my love; I may do that I shall be sorry for.
BRUTUS:	You have done that you should be sorry for. . . . I did send to you For certain sums of gold, which you denied me.
CASSIUS:	I denied you not.
BRUTUS:	You did.
CASSIUS:	I did not: he was but a fool That brought my answer back. Brutus hath riv'd my heart. A friend shall bear his friend's infirmities, But Brutus makes mine greater than they are.
BRUTUS:	I do not, till you practise them on me.
CASSIUS:	You love me not.
BRUTUS:	I don't like your faults.
CASSIUS:	A friendly eye could never see such faults.
BRUTUS:	A flatterer's would not.

(*Julius Caesar*, IV, 4)

2 Write an account, either in dramatic form or in reported speech, of an argument you have had recently with *either* a) a close friend, *or* b) a member of your family.

3 Continue the dialogue in the following dramatic situations. You may introduce one or two more characters, if you wish, but you are advised to continue the method of setting out the dialogue. (Avoid writing long passages of narrative!):

a) *The top-deck of a bus. Four teenage children, two boys and two girls, clatter up the stairs and fall laughing into the seats. They continue their conversation noisily to the embarrassment and annoyance of other passengers. After a time the conductor comes to collect the fares. He is a tall, well-built man, determined to exert his authority.*

CONDUCTOR: You're making too much noise. Sit down and behave yourselves. Where are you going?

JILL   *(cheekily)*: Where are we going?

JOHN   *(laughing)*: Home. Where are you going?

CONDUCTOR   *(loudly and seriously)*: Do you want to stay on this bus?

ANN   *(still giggling)*: Not particularly. I'll get off when I get there.

PHILIP: Stop it, can't you? The High Road, please.

CONDUCTOR: Right, all of you, off – now!

(The bus lurches and comes to a sudden stop.)

b) *One Saturday morning. The scene is a garage attached to a house on a private estate. The garage is filled with the usual junk – boxes, pieces of wood, coils of rope, garden chairs. Down one wall is a workbench littered with rools.*

   Dennis, in his forties, is busy at his workbench, muttering to himself and prodding an electric kettle with a screwdriver.

   DENNIS   *(frowning at the kettle)*: That goes in there . . . and then that one goes . . . through there to that one . . . which should join up with the other one. In which case . . .

   VERA   *(knocking gently on the garage door)*: Dennis . . . Dennis, dear, can you open the door for me, please? It's stuck again.

   DENNIS: Stand back. *(He heaves against the door which crashes open suddenly.)*

   VERA: John next door has come round to ask if you will hold his ladder while he takes his gutter down.

4 Report to a friend (using direct or indirect speech, or a mixture of the two) a conversation you overhead recently in a disco or a club about your friend's increasing unpopularity because of his or her increasingly superior attitude.

5 Write a short story which progresses almost completely in the form of a dialogue on one of the following:

   a) an archaeological discovery *or* a chance find;
   b) an accident on a bicycle;
   c) the recent death of a friend;
   d) a shop-lifting expedition *or* a false accusation.

6 Rewrite the report of the Nuremberg trial of Hermann Göring (given above in 3.8, pp. 41–2) retaining the detached point of view of the writer but replacing the reported speech by direct speech wherever possible.

7 Read 3.9 (pp. 42–3) above and then try to write a short narrative piece of verse entirely in the form of a dialogue which tells of an incident which affected you deeply.

8 Continue in an interesting way (by adding a further scene, if you wish) the conversation between Julie and Clive in 3.10, pp. 43–4.

9 To demonstrate the points of view of speakers and the interaction that exists between them, try to establish the other half of the following telephone conversation partly overhead recently in the office of the service manager in a garage. What attitudes are adopted by the speakers? How can you tell what the unseen speaker was saying? Is the other speaker a man or woman, old or young, working-class or middle class, educated or uneducated, and so on? What can you discover about him or her?

MANAGER:	Hello. Sungate.
SPEAKER B:	
MANAGER:	We've hit a spot of bother.
SPEAKER B:	
MANAGER:	It's not too bad. The gasket's gone. We've got to take the head off. Jags are not easy.
SPEAKER B:	
MANAGER:	Hard to say. About a hundred quid plus VAT.
SPEAKER B:	
MANAGER:	I know. But we hadn't taken it out on the road then.
SPEAKER B:	
MANAGER:	No, that was OK.
SPEAKER B:	
MANAGER:	Tomorrow night now.
SPEAKER B:	
MANAGER:	I can't guarantee it. Depends what else we find. Give us a ring about lunch-time.
SPEAKER B:	
MANAGER:	We can lend you one to pick them up from school.
SPEAKER B:	
MANAGER:	You can get it off the other chap's insurance.
SPEAKER B:	
MANAGER:	Yes.
SPEAKER B:	
MANAGER:	OK, then. Give us a ring tomorrow.

10 Both Charles Dickens (in *Great Expectations*) and Thomas Hardy (in a short story *The Distracted Preacher*) gave alternative endings

to their narratives. Some dramatists (e.g. Robert Bolt in *A Man For All Seasons* and Jean Anouilh in his work about St Joan, *L'Alouette*) also offered alternative endings to their plays. Bearing in mind the demands of plot and characterisation which must be maintained consistently, write an alternative final scene to a play (or a narrative) which you know well.

Reporting the facts

Consider the following newspaper report of an accident in Italy where a small hotel collapsed and several Britons on holiday miraculously escaped very serious injury. The point of view from which the accident is reported changes twice: first, from direct, objective, factual reporting in the third person to an eye-witness's/participant's account in the first person ('I . . . My . . . We . . .'); secondly, from the viewpoint of an eye-witness's account back again to an objective background comment in the third person.

In this report the emphasis is on established facts and so the selection of details and their arrangement are important:

Britons escape as Italian hotel collapses

British holiday-makers near Gozzano in Northern Italy escaped serious injury when their hotel in Bella Bernarda collapsed on Wednesday night.

First reports suggest that part of the mountainside below the hotel shifted because of recent rains and the subsequent earth-slip higher up the slope undermined the foundations. Although the hotel was full at the time, all the occupants escaped serious injury and were dug out by the rescue services which arrived quickly on the scene.

The British holiday-makers were:

Robert Llewellyn, 27, a lorry-driver, and his wife, Joan, 24, from Prestatyn, Clydd, North Wales; Mr Llewellyn's sister, Mrs Mary Templer, 23, and her husband, John, 24, from Hackney, London; Mrs Olga Betteson, 23, from Olney, Bucks; her husband, Tony, 24, was slightly hurt and is in hospital in Milan with a broken leg. Mr Llewellyn's father, Mr Harry Llewellyn, and his mother, Sophie, were amongst those treated for shock.

The accident occurred just before 3 am when everyone in the hotel was asleep. The holiday-makers were on a package-tour round Northern Italy organised by *Leisureplan Holidays* of Wrexham. They had planned to move on later this week to Florence and Venice.

The hotel had been used as a stop-over point for the tour company for the last five years. It was a small, family-run *albergo* with its own restaurant. A French family and two Italian business-men also staying overnight miracuously escaped, too. Mr Giuseppe Sottini, 57, and his wife, Nina, 56, the owners of the hotel, are being treated for shock in Milan.

Mrs Betteson told reporters: 'We went to bed about ten o'clock last night. The first we knew about it was when the ceiling fell on us and the bed shot down the floor into a big hole. The noise was terrible. There were dust and dirt everywhere. Tony was groaning I think he's got a broken leg. It was a mercy nobody was killed!'

Harry Llewellyn was too dazed to comment but his son, Robert, said: 'It seemed the whole world was coming to an end. There was an almighty crack and the sky opened up above us. Then the bed sank slowly into the restaurant below. What a mess! I thought I was having a nightmare at first.'

A French fifteen-year-old boy, Philippe Duparc, from Annecy in SE France, helped dig out the people trapped in their beds. His own family were badly shaken but unhurt. He said: 'I thought the mountain had descended. It was not very droll, I can tell you.'

Two years ago in Testa di Chambave, forty miles away from Wednesday's disaster, a similar land-slip destroyed a chalet-restaurant with the loss of two lives. The holiday firm had operated for the last twenty-five years without serious accident. Last night a representative of *Leisureplan Holidays* was flying out to see if other arrangements should be made for the British holiday-makers to continue their trip or fly home.

The audience at whom this report is directed is clear: a readership which wants the facts clearly set out but brought to life by one or two eye-witnesses' accounts.

The report of the same incident in another newspapers was given more dramatically with a greater emphasis on eye-witness accounts. The point of view changes rapidly from objective, third-person reporting to first person descriptions full of graphic detail. Notice particularly the use of emotive words and phrases: e.g. 'taken away in tears', 'the whole lot fell in', 'the floor went first', 'opened up like a tin can', 'a miracle', *etc.* and the individual experiences described in the minutest detail.

Going, Going, Gone! Hotel Collapses. British Holiday-makers Miss Death.

A peaceful holiday finished for some Britons on Wednesday night when their hotel collapsed in ruins at Bella Bernarda, N. Italy. Without warning at 3 am the whole building shook and slid down the mountainside in the Italian Alps. Miraculously everyone in the small family-run hotel escaped injury, although Mr Giuseppe Sottini, the owner, was found wandering an hour later in a nearby village:

'Nothing has ever happened to my family like this before. We are ruined. Last night we had everything. This morning nothing.'

He was taken away in tears and suffering from shock to a hospital in Milan where he is said to be recovering well.

A British lorry-driver, Robert Llewellyn, 27, and his newly married wife, Joan, 24, were on their honeymoon.

'This is something to tell our grandchildren,' he quipped. 'Fancy, the whole lot fell in on us! Joan said she thought the floor went first. We kept sliding for ages. Thank goodness we all got out safely – largely due to that French lad who dug people out with his bare hands.'

Philippe Duparc, 15, from the French mountain resort of Annecy in the Savoy Alps, was on holiday with his family in the hotel when the accident happened. He worked for hours helping people out of the rubble.

John Templer, 24, from Hackney, London, and his wife, Mary, 23, a teacher and the sister of Robert Llewellyn, were both saved by Philippe Duparc:

'He was ruddy marvellous,' said John Templer. 'He was the one who got things organised. The owner went off his head and walked round and round in circles gibbering all the time; Philippe got people out. It was funny, really. Bits of plaster came down on us like snow. Then there was a bang and the side wall opened up like a tin can. The bed tilted and Mary and I found ourselves in the kitchen, covered in pots and pans.'

Two other Britons were slightly hurt in the accident. Mrs Olga Betteson, 23, from Olney, Bucks, escaped with cuts and bruises, but her husband, Tony, 24, was taken to the Central Hospital in Milan with a broken leg.

Leisureplan Holidays, Ltd, of Wrexham, who arranged the holiday said last night: 'We are still trying to find out exactly what happened. The one thing we do know is that none of our holiday-makers was seriously hurt, although one has a broken leg. There will be an official inquiry by us and by the Italian authorities. Our main concern is to get our people home or on with their holiday – if that's what they want.'

Some of the members of the group are expected back later today at Gatwick Airport.

In a third newspaper account of the same incident, notice the frequent changes that occur in the point of view from which the report is given: from detached, observed, factual reporting to eye-witness accounts, to comments by the writer himself.

Honeymooners' roof falls in Britons avoid death in the Alps

JOHN ENDSLEIGH

Honeymooners, lorry-driver, Robert Lewellyn, 27, and his wife Joan, 24, who married last Saturday in Prestatyn, Clydd, N. Wales, got more than they bargained for on Wednesday night when their hotel collapsed at three in the morning in Bella Barnarda, N. Italy.

'All we wanted was a bit of peace,' said Robert. 'I want to get back home to Prestatyn,' said Joan. 'It's a wonder we weren't all killed.'

This was a family holiday planned over a year ago by Harry Llewellyn, 61, a construction engineer, and his wife, Sophie, 59, who are now recovering from shock. They booked a holiday in the Italian Alps with *Leisureplan Holidays*, of Wrexham for their son Robert and his then fiancée, Joan, and for their daughter Mary, 23, a teacher, and her husband, John Templer, 24, an estate agent. This was to have been the holiday of a lifetime. Robert and Joan meanwhile got married but kept the plans for the holiday.

John was concerned about Robert and Joan: 'Fancy! What a way to spend a honeymoon!' 'Ours was much quieter,' Mary added.

Two other Britons were in the hotel at the time: Tony Betteson, 24, from Olney, Bucks, finished his holiday in a Milan hospital nursing a broken leg, but his wife, Olga, 23, a hairdresser, escaped unhurt.

The hero of the night was a fifteen-year-old French boy, Philippe Duparc, from Annecy in the French Alps. He was staying with his family, who all escaped with minor shock. Philippe led the rescue by digging through the rubble with his bare hands.

'He was marvellous,' Joan Templer said. 'He just seemed to take control. He deserves a medal – the Croix de Guerre or something.'

Leisureplan Holidays, Ltd confirmed that their representatives had flown out from Birmingham last night:

'Holidaymakers are insured with us,' they said. 'They'll be compensated. We're just glad nobody was killed.'

This was the second hotel in the area to collapse because of a land-slip in recent years. I asked the local Italian tourist office to comment on this last night but they declinded until an investigation had been carried out.

Objective comment

4.2

Novelists and the writers of stories frequently make use of the objective point of view to unfold their narrative. Such an approach is now a convention in the writing of fiction and allows the writer to indulge in the most improbable fantasies, such as describing in detail the secret thoughts of their characters, without causing the reader to suspend his or her disbelief and to ask such questions as 'How could he know what Alice was thinking?' 'How could he know what Alice said when she was on her own?':

> 'Well', *thought Alice to herself*. 'After such a fall as this, I shall think nothing of tumbling down-stairs! How brave they'll all think me at home! Why, I wouldn't say anything about it, even if I fell off the top of the house!' (Which was very likely true.)
> Down, down, down. Would the fall never come to an end? '*I wonder how many miles I've fallen by this time?*' *she said aloud.* 'I must be getting somewhere near the centre of the earth. Let me see: that would be four thousand miles down, I think –' (for, you see, Alice had learnt several things of this sort in her lessons in the school-room). 'I wonder what Latitude or Longitude I've got to?' (Alice had not the slightest idea what Latitude was, or Longitude either, but she thought they were nice grand words to say.)

The intrusion of the author (with his own personal point of view in the remarks in brackets) runs the serious risk of destroying the illusion created by the third-person, objective narrator who knows everything.

4.3

Candidates in examinations are often asked to produce a short story. This is more difficult than it seems to many of the weaker candidates, who gladly rush into a narrative. They sometimes even manage to kill off the story-teller himself or herself at the end of the event and leave the reader puzzled about now the story ever came to be written down. *Such writing from the grave* strains the credulity a little!

> e.g. . . . He entered the room and confronted the enemy who stood pointing a pistol at him. He heard an explosion and felt himself dropping into a dark pool of silence. He was dead.

The situation is even worse, of course, for the candidate who has decided to use the personal approach and to write from the point of view of the first person:

> e.g. . . . I entered the room and confronted my enemy who stood pointing a pistol at me. I heard an explosion and felt myself dropping into a dark pool of silence. I was dead.

The third-person approach

4.4

Minutes of business meetings and reports are usually written in the third person; the device allows the writers to distance themselves from the events and to bring to the writing some appearance of objectivity.

> e.g. The following is from a school magazine's report of a Parents' Evening:

This year the Parents' Evening was held on Thursday, 29th November.

The Head in his report commented on the successful development of the sixth form. He had been pleased to see the way the first-year sixth had settled well into the disciplines of Advanced work and the way the second-year sixth had determination and well-balanced confident personalities. He devoted much of his attention to a discussion of the educational system of this country that fails to offer a university place to every young person capable of benefiting from a university course.

The guest speaker, Dr A. W. Newall, OBE, BSc, AMIEE, FInstP, Director of the Atomic Energy Research Establishment at Harwell, argued that science was not merely a classification of facts; curiosity and the language of science were not enough. A scientist needed a special quality of imagination and insight that would enable him or her to understand the significance of facts. Rutherford's genius, Dr Newall showed his audience, lay not in conducting experiments and obtaining a factual list of observations but rather in making an imaginative leap towards the truth . . .

The evening concluded with some very sensitive verse-speaking of Clive Sansom's *The Witnesses* under the direction of Mr Jones and *The Little Suite for Orchestra* by Malcolm Arnold played under the direction of the Head of the Music Department.

4.5   When reports are written in the first person, however, they carry the full weight of the writer's own conviction. Sometimes government reports use this technique to give the impression that a committee producing the report was united in its views and expected their opinions to be listened to:

We have suggested that those authorities with areas of immigrant settlement should maintain a continuous assessment of the language needs of immigrant pupils in their schools. For the most part these are not accurately assessed unless there is a member of the advisory staff with a major responsibility for immigrant education in the authority. We would strongly urge the appointment of advisers with special responsibility for the language development of immigrant children.

4.6   The most obvious dangers confronting candidates using a third-person point-of-view approach to their writing are the use of **the lifeless passive** and the moribund '**one**'. Consider the two following passages. Which of them conveys its meaning to the reader better, although both of them deal with objective factual reporting?

a) *One* **was overwhelmed** by the disaster. Pictures **were taken** of children without food. Lorries with food supplies **were attacked** by parents as soon as *one* saw them arrive. *One's* heart **was moved** with pity as the misery of the village **was calculated** by *one*.

b) The disaster overwhelmed me. I took pictures of children without food. Parents attacked the food-supply lorries as soon as they saw them arriving. My heart was moved with pity as I calculated the misery of the village.

Again, the point of view of the writer determines the impact the writing has.

4.7   It must not be assumed too readily that the objective third-person point of view is necessarily the best or the only approach to use in any one kind of writing.

The following topic was set in a recent examination as a continuous writing exercise:

Holiday snapshots and family photographs.

The **subject** was clearly enough defined. A possible context was given as an additional rubric: ('You may wish to describe the humour, excitement, boredom or embarrassment of taking and looking at such pictures'). The audience, or the reader for whom the writing is intended, was not specified, but presumably candidates would have directed it towards an unknown examiner or some member of the family or towards himself or herself. It was clearly important to establish the point of view of the writing, since its success would be judged largely by its impact on the reader.

It would have been possible to approach this topic from the viewpoint of someone interested in photography. The details given might have been presented objectively in the third person. Equally well, however, the writing in the third person might have been combined with dialogue or reported anecdotes and memories from friends, relatives or acquaintances. An immediate impact on the reader would have been established, however, by using a personal style of writing.

Consider the advantages of the following three openings:

a) 'Holiday snapshots for the family album are best avoided: they are difficult to take successfully and are tedious to look at as their colours fade and corners turn up . . .'
(Objective; third person.)

b) 'Photographs must be composed to be successful. The decapitated favourite aunt, the footless five-year-old, the small, blurred figure lost in a distant wilderness are familiar objects in the family album. I was once responsible for executing mother at Bognor Regis . . .'
(Objective and subjective mixed, using both the third person plus the personal, first person.)

c) 'Say *cheese*. No, not "gorgonzola" or "cheddar". Just *cheese* will do.'
   What a bore taking photographs really is! I hate the conventions, the posing, the inane grins, the mock laughter and the subsequent postmortems . . .
(Dramatic plus personal, first person.)

In all three, the writer's viewpoint is clear and there is some immediate contact with the reader. Before beginning, the writer must establish whether he or she will be a spectator or a participant *or* a spectator at one time and a participant at another.

Exercises

1 Consider the 'objective' reporting of a mass cycle-ride to Brighton given in two newspapers. Can you spot a fundamental difference between the two accounts?

LIFE CYCLE

More than 12,000 cyclists pedalled from London to Brighton yesterday to raise more than £100,000 for the British Heart Foundation.

LONDON–BRIGHTON CYCLE RALLY

About 12,000 cyclists took to their machines yesterday on the annual London–Brighton rally. Their sponsored ride was hoped to raise more than £100,000 for the British Heart Foundation. Large numbers turned out to welcome the riders at the end of their day's run. Most of them finished.

Write a report for a national newspaper of such an event, including as you do so some (possible) comments made by one or two competitors, an angry motorist who was held up by the cyclists, and the organiser of the event.

2 Rewrite from an objective point of view the following news report:

   a) *first*, in the style of the newspaper you are most familiar with, *and*

   b) *secondly*, as an article written by a Zimbabwe government official as a press release giving the facts to journalists to adapt as they wish for their own particular papers:

KILLED BY MOTHER ELEPHANT
by HUGH DAVIES in Harare

The goring to death by an elephant of one of Southern Africa's best known white hunters, Mr Ura de Woronin, 69, in the Zambezi Valley of northern Zimbabwe, has shocked and puzzled everyone who knew him.

   Russian-born Mr de Woronin was strolling back to his safari camp quarters one evening last week after supper when he came across a baby elephant. He tried to shoo it away, but the mother suddenly charged out of the surrounding bush, trumpeting angrily, and attacked him.

   A close friend, Mr Martin Rushmere, said that he knew the bush and its wild animals as well as anyone. 'We can only assume he didn't realise the mother was anywhere near. Otherwise he would have stayed well clear of the calf.'

   At the time of his death Mr de Woronin was a technical adviser on bushcraft and survival to the British film director Terry Bulley, who is producing a film on two children stranded in the bush after an air crash.

3 Write a narrative composition (in about 450 words) on *one* of the following from the point of view of the 'omniscient' author (*i.e.* one

who writes as if he knows every detail – even what his characters' innermost thoughts and feelings are):

    a) A night spent in a condemned cell with a prisoner awaiting execution at 8.00 a.m. the following morning.
    b) A morning when everything went wrong.
    c) A family argument.
    d) Trapped by one's past.
    e) A story ending, 'And she laughed all the way to the bank!'

4 Write a short story in 400–500 words, on *one* of the following topics, told from the personal viewpoint of the writer (using the first person 'I', 'we') but *which ends with the death of the writer*. Find a way to end the story which does not leave the reader asking, 'How could he have told the story if he dropped dead at the very end?'. (Try to avoid using 'the dream device', where the action turns out to be a dream after all.)

    a) My last Will and Testament.
    b) A day when fate finally struck.
    c) A noble struggle.
    d) Things that go bang in the night.
    e) The attack.

5   a) Write a report in about 350 words for *either* a school or college magazine *or* a local newspaper of a major public event held in your school or college.
    b) Write a detailed entry for a personal diary of the same event you described in the first part (a) of this exercise. *(Use about 250 words but make clear the point of view from which you are writing.)*

6 Write a report for the members of your class of a visit you made recently to *either* a job centre *or* a neighbouring school or college. (Select your facts and arrange them in an orderly manner. Once you have decided on your approach using either the 'objective' or the 'subjective' style, be sure to maintain it. Your report should be about 300 words in length.)

7   a) Read the following account of the way some Nazi leaders were sentenced to death at the end of the Nuremberg trial in 1946. It uses a third-person method of reporting, but some elements in it make the report emotional and reflect the writer's own implicit attitude and views. What are these elements?

NEMESIS

'On the counts of the Indictment on which you have been convicted the International Military Tribunal sentences you to death by hanging.'

Within an hour on the afternoon of October 1 Lord Justice Lawrence in these terse, grim words passed sentence of death on twelve of the leaders of the Third Reich: three others were sent to prison for life, and four were condemned to terms of from ten to twenty years' imprisonment. Three were acquitted, to the surprise of a good many people – though if there were to be acquittals, we always knew who they would be.

So, in the awsome serenity of the law, Nuremberg passed into history bearing the still breathless hopes of mankind that a decisive step forward had been taken in making the world secure from war.

This was by no means the first time that the rulers of a vanquished foe were made to pay with their lives. There was a time when their own people wreaked vengence upon them – a steep hill and a spiked barrel. But never before had they been summoned to the bar of the world's conscience to answer for the crime of aggressive war. Whatever may be said about Nuremberg in the years to come, never was a judgment so free of the blind vengeance of the victors. If they had to die they would die bravely, these tools of a lusting tyranny that had blotted out the sun for their generation and left behind the darkest vale of tears the world has known. 'Tode durch den Strang' – 'Death by the rope!' The words came to them in German through the headphones as each prisoner was brought up alone into the vast emptiness of the dock – the identical words pronounced by the Nazi People's Court upon the perpetrators of the July plot. They were uttered in translation by Captain Wolfe Frank, himself of German origin, who before departing from his country had watched the torchlight procession in Munich that had hailed Hitler's coming to power. A strange turn of the wheel that he was now to utter the words that set the seal on Hitler's little day.

b) Rewrite the report of the Nuremberg Trial's conclusion given above from the personal viewpoint of the writer, using the first person and making explicit some of his own implicit attitudes and views. (Do not add details of your own but keep to the facts and their order given in the passage.)

8 Write three possible opening paragraphs of a composition as part of a public examination, on one of the following topics:

a) Memories of early childhood.
b) A good time was had by all.
c) The opposite sex.

Your three paragraphs should respectively take up the following viewpoints so that the reader is in no doubt about the angle from which you, as the writer, are approaching the topic:

i)   objective; third person;
ii) objective and subjective mixed, using both third and first persons;
iii) dramatic and personal.

9 From the pages of a recent newspaper take a major news item which reported simply, factually, and objectively an incident involving at least three people. Rewrite the article for the same newspaper, but approach the reporting from a personal point of view; you may include some direct quotations from those people involved, if you wish.

10 From the pages of a recent newspaper take a major news item which reported subjectively, with the help of direct quotations from those people involved, a major accident. Rewrite the article for the same newspaper but approach the reporting from an objective point of view. Use reported speech if you wish to include comments from those involved.

5 The Topic

'When *I* use a word,' Humpty Dumpty said, in rather a scornful tone, 'it means just what I choose it to mean — neither more nor less.'

Lewis Carroll, *Alice Through the Looking Glass*

A major part of the skill in using the English language lies in understanding the concepts to be expressed: 'Take care of the sense and the sounds will take care of themselves' (The Duchess in *Alice's Adventures in Wonderland*).

Clarity and appropriateness

5.1 These are two of the fundamental qualities of 'good' English; it is these qualities which account for differences in English which exist in subjects across the school curriculum.

It is not always appropriate in creative or poetic writing for a word to carry only one meaning; indeed, ambiguities (double or multiple meanings) often account for its richness:

e.g. 'The dawn stole up on the day, like a thief in the night.'

In scientific or legal writing, however, it would be a hindrance to understanding and communication if words carried a multiplicity of interpretations:

e.g. in Chemistry words such as *mix, combine, react, blend,* need to be used carefully if the concepts underlying physical and chemical changes are to be described accurately. There is a critical distinction in chemistry between a mixture and a compound just as there is a critical distinction in law between a *Crown Court* and a *County Court.*

5.2 Nevertheless, a sensitive user of English, whether in writing or speaking, will be aware of, be able to recognise, and respond to what is appropriate to a particular use or a particular subject. The term 'registers' is sometimes applied to the levels on which the language is used appropriate to particular contexts (see p. 5).

Take, for example, the following three pieces of writing and try to determine which is appropriate in its register for each of the following subjects: Economics; History; Religious Studies. What features helped you make your choice?

a) The early decision by the government to put into practice the cuts in the dole was a cause of deep-felt resentment among unemployed workers, who experienced a further decline in their already sparse living conditions. In addition a means test was imposed, by which an unemployed man's benefit would be lowered if other members of his household were in employment.

b) The effect of unemployment on a man and his family is to dehumanise him. He loses his self-respect and so begins to despair of any eternal plan for his life. Man cannot live by bread alone but the fundamental means of existence are essential to personal dignity. One man unemployed is a challenge to the thousands in employment. One man's humiliation diminishes us all.

c) Total unemployment has been found to move up and down in quite well-defined cycles in line with changes in demand and output. Structural unemployment arises when a permanent decline occurs in the demand for certain types of goods and services. In Britain industries which have experienced structural unemployment include ship-building, cotton textiles and coal-mining.

5.3 It is not possible to list qualities always appropriate to one subject area rather than another, since the language uses are not always discrete. Minor variations or adaptations in the language might easily allow switches between registers to be easily accomplished and the communication to remain unobstructed.

5.4 Nevertheless, there are some very specific subject skills related to different subjects in the curriculum (see also Chapter 8, pp. 106–23) and it is important that these subject-related skills expressed in specific language are recognised and mastered. In Physics, for example, language appropriate to calculation, classification, accurate description, and clear explanation needs to be cultivated but in all sciences technical vocabulary and expressions must be learnt.

5.5 Although it is not easy to pinpoint the essential features of good English required for a particular subject area or set of subjects, the topic and the subject matter to be used will impose their own requirements on register and style.

To see that this is so, consider the description of a piece of agricultural machinery written in verse or the description of a scientific experiment written up in elaborate, often figurative English. The marriages of topic and style are uneasy:

a)   THE STEAM THRESHING MACHINE
    Flush with the pond the lurid furnace burned
    At eve, while smoke and vapour filled the yard;
    The gloomy winter sky was dimly starred
    The fly-wheel with a yellow murmur – turned;
    While, ever rising on its mystic stair
    In the dim light, from secret chambers borne,
    The straw of harvest, severed from the corn,
    Climbed and fell over, in the murky air.

b) The confusions for the reader in the following description (from the same period) of an experiment arise not so much from the scientific observations described but from the language itself with its mixture of colourful images and humdrum comparisons:

> And now with regard to the melting of ice. On the surface of a flask containing a freezing mixture we obtain a *thick fur of hoar-frost*. Sending a beam through a water-cell, *its luminous waves* are concentrated upon the surface of the flask. Not a spicula* of the frost is dissolved. We now remove the water-cell, and in a moment a *patch of frozen-fur as large as half-a-crown* is melted. Hence, inasmuch as the full beam produces this effect, and the luminous part of the beam does not produce it, we fix upon the dark portion of the melting of the frost.
>
> As before, we clench this inference by concentrating the dark *waves* alone upon the flask. The first is *dissipated* exactly as it was by the full beam. These effects are rendered strikingly visible by darkening with ink the freezing mixture within the flask. When *the hoar-frost* is removed, the blackness of the surface from which it had been melted comes out in strong contrast with *the adjacent snowy whiteness*. When the flask itself, instead of the freezing mixture, is blackened, *the purely luminous waves* being absorbed by the glass, warm it. The glass *reacts* upon the frost and melts it. *Hence* the wisdom of darkening, instead of the flask itself, the mixture within the flask.

Clear? The language (especially those words and phrases italicised) obscures rather than clarifies what was a simple piece of scientific observation!

    * *a spike or splinter*

The inappropriateness of some language for a specific context can become even more ludicrous in official documents or letters. The following letter was awarded a booby prize (two pounds of the best, ripe, Lancashire tripe) in the Plain English Awards, 1981, Competition organised by the Plain English Campaign and the National Consumer Council. *The Daily Telegraph* published it as 'a winning entry':

A Letter from the

Travellers' Insurance Association

We would advise that our policy does exclude a contingency consequent upon a condition which is receiving or awaiting treatment at the date of issue of policy.

We would therefore advise that the person who had a heart operation in 1963 is not receiving any of the forementioned as she will be covered for that condition under the policy.

If the lady is receiving any of the aforementioned the policy only excludes her for a contingecy upon that particular condition.

We still wish to offer her the cover of the rest of the policy including medical and other expenses and the cancellation or curtailment due to any unforeseen condition for which she is not receiving any medication or treatment for.

We hope this clarifies the situation.

(The last sentence must surely be ironic!)

5.7

Nevertheless, it is possible to notice some of the more obvious features of good English related to the **kind** of subject matter it is expressing. (The following examples are intended to be illustrative rather than exhaustive.)

'Business' or 'commercial' English

5.8

Letters to or from a firm, applications for posts, reports on new projects and other forms of English used in business or commerce are marked by:

a) *brevity* (Express yourself with economy.)
b) *relevance* (Keep to the point.)
c) *clarity* (Say what you mean and mean what you say.)
d) *formality* (Avoid over-familiarity; guard your objectivity.)
e) *conventions* (Observe scrupulously the niceties of the 'register', the setting-out of addresses and references, and polite – but not obsequious – expression.)

Above all, it is important to avoid clichés (over-worked, phrases), stilted expressions, and outmoded vocabulary: *e.g. inst.* (this month), *ult.* (last month), *prox.* (next month), *re* (with reference to); *we beg to inform you*; *we humbly acknowledge*, etc.

Brevity

A busy office may have dozens or hundreds of letters to deal with every day; it is important that correspondence should be as brief as possible – without sacrificing clarity or polite conventions.

Relevance

This calls for the careful selection of material and the perhaps ruthless exclusion of any comments which do not have a direct bearing on the matter under consideration. Extraneous material or comments merely blur the issue and distort the focus.

Clarity

This is the most difficult quality to achieve. Brevity and relevance will contribute to clarity, but (i) choice of appropriate vocabulary (the simpler the better), (ii) the appropriate use of jargon (technical terms used accurately within a context), (iii) simple constructions (avoiding long complex sentences with too many qualifications of meaning), and (iv) the avoidance of flamboyant figurative language (comparisons, contrasts, exaggerations etc.) will help to make what you are saying clear. (Where is the irony in *this* sentence?)

Formality

It is important to establish from the outset what point of view to adopt as a writer and to maintain it. The decision about the point of view will, of course, depend too on the nature of the topic and the relationship with the person being addressed ('the audience'). It is usually best in business English to use either the third person (*he, she, it, they*) or, if the writer is speaking on behalf of his or her firm or company, the first person plural (*we*). Above all, once the stance or point of view has been decided, it should be maintained.

Conventions

There are well-recognised conventions used in business English. These include:

a) the setting-out correctly of letters. *The address of the sender* is placed at the top right-hand corner of the page; each line of the address needs a comma at its end, except the last which requires a full-stop. *The date* is placed under the address and is normally written in full e.g. 1 June 1984. *The name(s) of the person(s) to whom the letter is sent* is placed on the left-hand side of the page, starting on the line below that used for the date. The normal *form of address* is 'Dear Sir' or 'Dear Madam', unless the person is well-known to the writer, when 'Dear Mr X' or 'Dear Miss/Ms/ Mrs X' may be used. On the line following the form of address *reference numbers and details* should be given and underlined: e.g. *Your Ref. XHJ/30/29; Our Ref. MB/RS/101*. At the end of the letter *the conclusion* should be 'Yours faithfully' or, if the form of address was 'Dear Sir' or 'Dear Madam', it may be 'Yours truly'. (NB. The capitalisation of 'Yours' and the absence of an apostrophe; the small letter for 'faithfully' or 'truly' and the use of the comma.) The letter should be **signed** with a *legible signature*.
b) **The correct lay-out of reports.** Reports may be presented as a formal/business letter or in a formal manner which sets out:

> *the source of the report;*
> *the destination* (the name of an individual, committee, firm, or organisation);
> *the date;*
> *the subject of the report of a heading;*

the terms of reference;
the constitution of the committee, working party, etc.;
the procedure used to complete the work undertaken;
the findings;
the conclusion(s);
the recommendations;
signature(s) with the status of the sender (e.g.
'Chairman') clearly specified.

'Legal' English

5.9   The kind of English used in legal documents (e.g. wills, insurance policies, court papers, etc., is marked by:

a) brevity;
b) clarity;
c) jargon.

Documents of a legal kind attempt to avoid all ambiguities and to leave only one interpretation of the meaning possible. Since punctuation as an element additional to the words themselves can determine meaning, legal documents often avoid using any punctuation at all, apart from the occasional capital letter.

e.g. Amount assured £3,000 (three thousand pounds) in the first year decreasing at the end of each completed year of assurance by the sum by which principal under a mortgage effected at the date of the policy for an amount equal to the sum assured would have decreased during that year if repayable over a period of 20 years by equal monthly quarterly or half yearly instalments comprising principal and interest on the outstanding principal at the rate of $8 \cdot 5$ per cent per annum without profits

Jargon, although sometimes used in the same sense as 'slang' (*Chambers Twentieth Century Dictionary* gives this as one of its main meanings), properly refers to a trade dialect. Lawyers, doctors, teachers, carpenters – and the members of any trade or profession – use vocabulary peculiar to themselves. A car workshop manual or a monthly specialist magazine aimed at computer-controllers will contain its own special use of language. Far from being careless, imprecise, and slovenly language, trade jargon is economical and accurate in its usage.

Language used in science

(See also **Chapter 8**, pp. 106–23.) This 'kind' of English is usually marked by:

a) brevity;
b) clarity;
c) selectivity/order;
d) accuracy in recording observed facts;
e) jargon.

Frequently, the 'audience' is so specialised that the area within which communication can take place is taken for granted.

> e.g. The 630 ECS can print special symbols and graphics which are not available on standard alphanumeric print wheels. Two of the special 192 character print wheels are currently available, one for scientific and technical purposes and the other for multilingual and teletext applications. The scientific and technical daisywheel contains a 12 pitch elite alphanumeric typeface plus 96 matching scientific symbols and allows a further 165 characters to be constructed. The multilingual daisywheel contains 10 pitch pica alphanumeric typeface and 96 symbols and graphics characters and allows a further 173 characters to be constructed. The latter daisywheel will support 33 of the languages used in western industrialised nations. Additional print wheels are currently under development to support users employing printers in other specialised applications.

One of the major difficulties of the language of science for students lies in the area of vocabulary, particularly those words in the following categories:

a) **Specialised words; jargon:** *e.g. allotrophy, carbonate, catalysis, chlorophyll, efflorescence, electrolysis, hydrolysis, manganese, molecule, titration; capillarity, hydrophone, node, osmosis; logarithm, maxima and minima, quadratic; specific gravity, etc.*
b) **Common words with specialised meanings:** *e.g. analysis, atom, chemical change, combustion, compound, elements, equation, formula, hypothesis, mixture, radical, solution; cohesion, elasticity, gas, liquid, resonance, solid, velocity; compound, equation, prime, hardware, etc.*
c) **Specialised words that have become common in usage:** *e.g. bicarbonate, calcium, cast iron; pasteurised; anaesthetic, diphtheria, vaccinate, vitamins; dynamo, ultra-violet; creosote, stratosphere; psychopathic.*

d) **New coinages:** *e.g. horsepower, emulsion; floppy disc, cellophane, rayon, nylon; videotape; topstore, lympet logger, ergomatic, strobe, microlink, thermal paper, glass optics, teletext.*

Language used in the media

5.11   The media include radio, TV, newspapers, magazines, propaganda. Here definitions of 'kinds' of language break down, since there is no such thing as a single 'register' or 'language' for the news or the communication of ideas to the public in general. On the one hand there are those who think that the media should be impartial: on the other hand there are those who freely argue that the very act of selection destroys impartiality and leads to *propaganda*; often what is not included in a news report is as important as what *is* included. Between those two extremes lies the whole spectrum of language-use by the media.

5.12   An analysis of an important news item from a national newspaper will illustrate some of the ways in which information is given one emphasis rather than another. At the end of August 1983, a South Korean Boeing 747 was reported to have been shot down by Soviet fighters over Moneron Island as it flew over Russian territory; all 269 members of the crew and passengers lost their lives. The incident formed the major news item in British national newspapers during the first week of September. On 6 September 1983, *The Daily Telegraph* reported at length as its major news item a speech by President Reagan in which he condemned the Russian act as one of 'savagery' and 'barbarism'. The report of the speech and of related items occupied some 126 cm of column space on the front and back pages, but only 4·5 cm of the main report were devoted to the fact that an American RC–135 spy plane was also in the area at the time; a fuller and more detailed discussion of the possible confusion by the Russians of a Boeing 747 and an RC–135 was, however, given considerable prominence *inside* the paper on page 4. A reader would have needed to read *both* articles and make connections between them in order to draw his or her own conclusions.

5.13   It is hard to achieve objective reporting of a news item; often the slanting of the information is subtle and very effective. On 1 February 1979 the BBC TV programme *Nine O'Clock News* reported on a serious public service workers' dispute which jeopardised the National Health Service for a time. The opening of the report is quoted and commented on as follows by John Hartley in *Understanding News* (in the series 'Studies in Communication', Methuen, 1982, pp. 119–20):

The 'report'

Here at home the dispute by public service workers is still spreading.

Half the hospitals in England and Wales and some in Scotland can now open their doors only to emergency cases.

Apart from the hospitals the strike is affecting more ambulance services and schools, as well as water and sewerage workers.

In the Commons the Prime Minister urged the hospital ancillary workers to 'go back to work' while negotiations could continue on what he called 'a proper basis'.

The Prime Minister also said: 'It is not acceptable in any community that sick human beings, whether adults or children, should have their food denied to them and proper attention forbidden to them'.

Comment

'Initially, then, the story concerns a dispute between workers in hospital, the ambulance service, schools, water and sewerage services, and their employers: the area health authorities, local education authorities, water authorities, etc. But already a *structured* absence is built into the news-framing of the story. At first sight it looks like a grammatical error, but '. . . the dispute *by* . . .' is ideologically very productive. Disputes are by definition *between* two people or parties: it takes two to tangle. The framing of the story as a dispute *by* just one group signifies the public service workers *alone* as the initiators of negative action. The employers simply disappear from the bulletin, apart from two references to 'hospital authorities' being 'able to keep essential services open', or 'being forced to refuse all but emergencies'.

The omission or inclusion of details forms, therefore a very significant 'slanting' of a news item.

5.14

The slanting of information, coupled with skilled rhetorical tricks can lead to very effective propaganda. An outstanding example of such manipulation of facts and audience occurred in the speech of Dr Joseph Goebbels, Hitler's Minister for Propaganda during the 1939–45 war, to a vast – and selected – audience in the *Sportpalast*, following the capitulation of the German Sixth Army at Stalingrad in 1942. The defeat had been reported on the German radio as a *Sondermeldung* (Special Announcement) accompanied by muffled drums and the national anthem and followed by a three-minute silence. Two weeks afterwards, Dr Goebbels made his speech to show that Germany was far from defeated. He put ten rhetorical questions to his audience; he pledged 'Total War' and his listeners rose to their feet and echoed his pledge without hesitation. His words were clearly calculated to stir his listeners:

> Two thousand years' constructive work by western humanity is in danger. Total war is therefore the need of the hour, for a danger recognised soon becomes a danger averted . . . The most radical is today just radical enough; the most total is today just total enough . . . It is time to take off the kid gloves and bind the fist. German men, to your weapons! German women, to work! . . . Do you want total war, do you want it, if necessary, more total and more radical than we can even imagine today? Is your faith in the Führer greater, more confident, and more unshakable today than it has ever been?

The audience rose as one in a frenzy of affirmation; the orator's success was total.

Language used in translations

5.15

To translate effectively from one language to another it is necessary to understand idiomatic usages within both languages. Such usages often embody national attitudes and reflect national assumptions about life, customs, habits, and moral and social values. It is also necessary to have control over vocabulary and language structure; a language can hardly ever be translated directly on a word-to-word basis. Consider for example, the following extract from a travel booklet issued by the Société Nationale des Chemins de Fer Français (SNCF), the French National Railway Company. It is easy to see what is meant, but the translation into English of French vocabulary and structures results in a passage that is not English.

> Town, seaside resort and seaport, an agglomeration of 40,000 inhabitants, DIEPPE is situated two hours by rail or road from Paris.
> The 'Grande Rue', the 'Puits Sale' and the 'Quais', the Sea Front are the elected places of Tourism. 'What a loveliness, and how gay it is there!' That's always the exclamation made by people coming to Dieppe for the first time.
> A special note has to be made to its high renowned restaurant 'L'Horizon', with its panoramic sight, a superb play-room

(theatre, cinema, music-hall) the ball-room 'The Club' – the saloons of the Cercle with 'Roulette', 'Baccara' and 'Boule' gamblings.

London/Paris through DIEPPE is the most direct way.

Dieppe always is worth a stop.

(*Guide Information*, Car-Ferry 'Valençay', 1965–6) SNCF

There is some direction of the writing – towards the potential visitor; the topic is clear – the attractions of Dieppe as a stopping-off town; the context is obvious – holidays and tourism. Yet the passage fails to achieve its apparent intention of attracting visitors since it ignores the idiom and structures of English.

Idiom, in the final analysis, cannot be translated literally from one language to another. A glance at some examples will immediately make this point clear.

English: She has other fish to fry.
French: Elle a d'autres chats à fouetter (*literally*, 'She has other cats to flog').
English: He has bats in the belfry.
German: Er hat Raupen im Kopfe (*literally*, 'He has worms in the head').

Structure, idiom, and vocabulary have all collapsed in the following passage taken from the wrapper on an imported cello string:

BOWED UNDER

The wrapper on an imported cello string read, in English: 'Thanks to this type of metal strings, it has been possible to achieve both the switness of sound and the softness, to fell that, one can recall the bowel stirrings of the past, but this type far better than the latter owing to the promptness in emission and the ready and stable tuning.'

Language used in advertisements

To make a successful advertisement a writer needs to:

a) select the facts to be stressed;
b) make an immediate impact on the reader/listener;
c) produce a memorable phrase or two;
d) lead the audience to make easy and pleasurable associations between the product and their own experience.

5.16

Selection, impact, recall, and **association** are sometimes linked with word-play and lead to new word-formations:

> e.g. 'Drinka Pinta – Quencha Thirst.'

> 'Bodyguards cost less than excorts' (Volvo advertisements stressing the protective body shell of their new model, Volvo 340 Hatchback)

Language used in politics

5.17

The treatment of a topic by politicians in order to leave themselves an escape route in the future, should they be closely questioned or called to account, frequently leads to deliberate ambiguity and evasiveness. It is often amazing just how little can be said at such length by a politician seeking to evade a point. The introductions to replies to 'difficult' questions often give away the fact that a precise answer will not be forthcoming:

> 'Before I answer your question, let me say that. . . .'
> 'I don't know about that, but I must stress that. . . .'
> 'Let me give you some facts. . . .'
> 'Our record speaks for itself. When the other party was in power, they. . . .'
> 'I'll come to that in a moment. What is important is that. . . .'
> 'Let me ask you a question. . . .'
> 'The point you make is interesting, but a more interesting point is that. . . .'

The vocabulary used by politicians often shifts its ground very easily so that words lose their normal associations and take on meanings that only the user seems to understand. Some examples of such 'slippery' words used in political contexts are: *democracy, monetarism, left/ right, exploitation, redeployment, defence, social justice, nationalisation, cuts, socialism, recovery, aid, military adviser, reactionary.*

Exercises

1 Look up the following *ten* words in a good dictionary. From the definitions given for each, find a specialised meaning of the word used in a particular profession; copy out the meaning and state the profession which uses it specifically with that meaning; then use

the word in a sentence of your own to show you understand the specialised, technical use of the word:

a) *acid*; b) *backcloth*; c) *to blunge*; d) *conveyance*; e) *to develop*; f) *diaphragm*; g) *dissect*; h) *hardware*; i) *strategy*; j) *to stream*.

2 Using most of the facts in the passage below, write articles for publication in:

a) a history textbook for use with pupils preparing for a CSE or GCE examination in history;
b) a church guidebook feature intended for tourists, tracing the early origins of the building.

'Account of Works at the Church of Westminster from Christmas in this year (1269) to the feast of the Purification of the Virgin in the fifty-fifth year (1270).'
Account total: £1,361 3s. 1½d.
And in marble, free-stone as well from Caen as from Reigate, flints, plaster, chalk, carriage of the aforesaid £485 12. 9d. And in great timber, boards, rafters, as well as oak as of alder, laths, hurdles, rods, grease, glue, and other small necessary things for the said works, as in the said particulars, £54 15s. 11½d. And in lead, iron, steel, coal, brushwood for making the iron-work, locks, cords, glass, wax, pitch and other necessaries for the glass windows, and for making cement, canvas for closing the windows of the aforesaid church, with the carriage thereof, £140 14s. 0d. And in hollowed tiles, litter, stubble for covering the walls of the same church, £4 11s. 4½d. And in gold in leaf and enamel, divers colours, and other necessaries for the pictures of the tomb in which reposes the body of the blessed Edward, and for the painting of the figures in the said church £32 16s. 1½d. Wages of masons and other works £670 5s. 10½d.
(Pipe Roll 54 Henry III AD 1269–70)

3 Which of the two following extracts is more appropriate to a student's biology notebook which he is drawing up as part of his work towards a final examination? Can you isolate the qualities which make one less appropriate than the other? There are some very marked differences.

How to set up a wormery

a) I fetched a bucket of soil and a cup. A jar of sand and some chalk. I fetched a wormery glass which you can see through. I made layers of soil then sand and then powdered chalk . . . I continued like that. Then I put some water in it. I have marked with biro where the water ran. Then I placed four worms in the wormery. They did not stir when they were on top of the soil but later they will.

I put the wormery into a dark cupboard which is closed.

b) A large glass was filled with alternating layers of soil, sand, and powdered chalk and then filled with water to a line drawn in biro. Four worms were placed in the glass which was then stored in a dark cupboard for later observation.

4 Write up the most interesting experiment you have ever done in *either* Physics, *or* Chemistry, *or* Biology, *or* Geology for:

a) your own personal notebook recording what you did in the science subject;

b) an answer to a question set as part of a CSE or GCE (Ordinary Level) examination.

(Make sure that you use an appropriate level of language; you should use diagrams if they make your account clearer.)

5 Re-write the following passage intended to explain the ideas to an ordinary member of the public who has no knowledge of Sociology. (You will need to do some preliminary work with a dictionary in order to disentangle the meaning of the jargon before you begin. The basic ideas expressed are really quite simple, in spite of the language used.)

> Human expressivity is capable of objectivation, that is it manifests itself in products of human activity that are available both to their producers and to other men as elements of a common world. Such objectivations serve as more or less enduring indices of the subjective processes of their producers, allowing their availability to extend beyond the face-to-face situation in which they can be directly apprehended.

6 Write a formal report for the Head of your school or college of a meeting called and conducted by members of the final year of their course to consider the poor conditions in which they have been expected to work. (See 5.8, pp. 66–8, for the requirements of a 'formal' report.)

7 a) Write a formal letter to the insurance company responsible for the paragraph set out as an example in 5.9 above, p. 68, asking them to explain in simple terms how it would apply to a young couple about to buy their own house for the first time.

b) Draft the formal reply that the insurance company might have sent to the young couple in response to such a letter.

8 Write a formal letter of application for the following advertised post. (Bear in mind the need to be *brief, clear, relevant,* and *formal* and to use the correct conventions for such a letter; see 6.8, p. 67.)

JOB

CENTRE

Apprentice lion-tamer required.
Age 16—20.
Man or woman.

APPLY:
Manager, Star Circus Ltd.,
Dudley,
West Midlands.
(Ref. AZ/101.)

---

9 Make a list of ten words (*with their meanings defined*) used in a specialised way in a hobby (e.g. photography, computers, pottery, horse-riding) or in an academic subject in which you are especially interested.

10 The following words have become commonly used in English and do not always bear the meanings they had when they were originally introduced into the language. With the help of a good modern dictionary make a list of (a) their original meanings, and (b) their common meanings today:

i) *taboo;* ii) *juggernaut;* iii) *placebo;* iv) *punk;* v) *blitz;* vi) *cast iron;* vii) *snorkel;* viii) *robot;* ix) *zombie;* x) *broadcast.*

11 Using your knowledge of the elements that make up the vocabulary of English and/or your knowledge of other languages, invent *ten* new words you would like to see in English to cover facts, ideas, feelings, situations, inventions, *etc.* for which no word currently exists. (Be prepared to explain and justify your new 'coinages'.)

A discussion exercise

12 Consider the following two passages carefully. They are taken from reports in *The Times* of the manifestos of the Labour and Conservative parties before the 1983 General Election; such statements are designed to attract votes by setting out future policies clearly and persuasively. How precise were the promises made?

How unambiguous were the undertakings? How did the vocabulary of each statement imply criticism of the other party's policies?

a) We will begin to rebuild British industry, working within a new framework for planning and industrial democracy. We will:

Agree a new national economic assessment, setting out the prospects for growth in the economy.

Prepare a five-year national plan, in consultation with unions and employers.

Back up these steps with a new National Investment Bank, new industrial powers, and a new Department for Economic and Industrial Planning.

Repeal Tory legislation on industrial relations and make provisions for introducing industrial democracy.

Begin the return to public ownership of those public industries sold off by the Tories.

b) Over the past four years, this country has recaptured much of her old pride. We now have five great tasks for the future. They are:

To create an economy which provides stable prices, lasting prosperity and employment for our people;

To build a responsible society which protects the weak but also allows the family and the individual to flourish;

To uphold parliamentary democracy and strengthen the rule of law;

To improve the quality of life in our cities and countryside;

To defend Britain's freedom, to keep faith with our allies in Europe and in Nato, and to keep the peace with justice.

13 Listen to tonight's main news bulletins on *one* of the BBC television channels *and* on *one* of the Independent television channels:

a) make a list of news items included on both channels;
b) make a list of news items included on one channel but not on the other;
c) try to describe any significant 'slanting' of the news you spotted on both channels;
d) write a short paragraph which sets out to explain how the personality of the newscaster affected your response to the news items.

14 Compare the reports in recent editions of *at least two* major national newspapers of an important incident. By a) investigating what they have in common; b) noticing what one includes and the other omits; and c) analysing the kinds of language each uses (e.g. jargon, dialogue, comment, point of view, 'loaded' vocabulary), write a statement for inclusion in a third newspaper about the intention of the editors in including such a news report.

15 Write a speech by someone interested in scientific research on the subject of 'The need to experiment on animals' to be delivered to a group representing ecology and conservation interests who seriously doubt such a need.

16 Write a speech you will give shortly in a school or college which is intended to convince a group of eighteen-year-old boys and girls that they should accept the views you present on:

    a) a topic you hold very strong opinions about;
    b) a topic you secretly have doubts yourself about;
    c) a topic you really are opposed to but prefer not to show your true feelings.

17 Write and design an advertisement to be included in a national paper which is intended to sell large quantities of *one* of the following:

    a) miniatures of the Eiffel Tower in 18-caret gold;
    b) a new-design of mousetrap;
    c) sewer-cleaning equipment;
    d) kilts to tourists from overseas;
    e) fragments of pottery and glass collected from the municipal rubbish-tip.

6 The Context

The situation in which a speaker or a writer uses English will help to determine some of the features of the language he or she uses; it is not possible to define in exact terms the kind of language that ought to be used in any particular situation, since the speaker or the writer is not a linguistic prisoner unable to make free choices. The style(s) chosen from an individual's store of language should, however, be appropriate to the complex factors which go to make up the situation or context in which he or she wants to use English.

Some of these factors are considered later in this chapter (pp. 85–9), but it should be remembered that the **context** involves a subtle interplay between all of them; if one factor is changed it affects the balance within the context and the 'style' of the writer or speaker would need to alter to remain *appropriate*.

6.1 **Appropriateness** in the use of English whether written or spoken involves not only an awareness of 'context' but also a recognition of a) *register* and b) *conventions* in the language.

a) The term **register** has already been discussed in chapter 1 (see **1.8** above). There it was shown that register is often determined by the context or situation in which the speaker or writer imagines or finds himself or herself to be. Love-letters, a letter from a bank manager to a client with an overdraft, a statement in a court of law, a complaint to a company about a faulty product, or a holiday postcard to a friend will all demand appropriate 'registers'. Similarly, a description of a sunset or of an encounter with a ghost or a visit to a disco written as part of an examination exercise will require an appropriate level of language usage. Sometimes a speaker or a writer will deliberately use the wrong 'register', one quite inappropriate to the context, in order to create a humorous or satirical or embarrassing effect.

b) An awareness, too, of the **conventions** required by the language for particular contexts is essential for good writing or speaking. Varieties of English according to the topic ('legal', 'official', 'scientific', 'literary', 'journalistic', 'political' – see **Chapter 5**, pp. 62–74) follow patterns of approach, vocabulary, structures and punctuation that have grown into readily recognisable conventions, perhaps over many years. For example, a visit to a doctor to describe the symptoms of a possible illness will require a different level of language usage from that employed in a conversation between two old friends who meet in a bar after two years without having seen each other. Probably we never need to acquire control over more than a few 'varieties', but it is useful to be able to recognise them and to be sensitive to the ways in which they are used. Whatever the variety, *the clear communication of meaning on the level appropriate to the topic and the audience should be the aim of the person using the language*; he or she should be able to operate within the traditions of the chosen variety of English being used and avoid becoming unintentionally obscure.

In considering some of the conventions used it will be useful to bear in mind the following headings: a) Approach; b) Vocabulary; c) Structures; and d) Punctuation.

6.2

Approach

The purpose for which a piece of writing is intended will do much to determine its style. 'Legal' English, for example, aims to avoid ambiguities at all costs; the terms of a will must be unambiguously set out; a contract must be incapable of being misunderstood or misinterpreted. Such English tends to rely on specialised words and formulas rather than on punctuation to establish meaning.

On the other hand, it is often the method of 'political' writing deliberately to avoid too precise a use of the language. Journalists and commentators have long memories and delight in quoting a politicians' speech, often out of context, many months later in order to embarrass him or her. If the remarks are capable of several interpretations, not only will a wider audience be pleased, but also the politician can still persuade the uncritical listener or reader without leaving himself vulnerable later on.

'Literary' English sometimes draws its strength from the fact that it can be interpreted on several levels of meaning at the same time: comparisons, colourful imaginative words, experiments in new structures to surprise, amuse, analyse, or persuade often abound. In such language a deliberately 'ambiguous' use of English can enrich, rather than obscure, meaning. (NOTE: *Ambiguous* can mean 'of double meaning' as well as obscure.)

(See also **Chapter 8** where different categories of writing are discussed in detail.)

Vocabulary

Conventions have arisen within some varieties of English which demand the use of specialised vocabulary to avoid ambiguities or unnecessary length. Scientific, legal, and commercial varieties often use *jargon* to achieve this concise expression. The word 'jargon' has already been discussed in **Chapter 5** (see **5.9**, p. 68). Even those who write on language itself very often fall back on the jargon of their own subject to explain meaning concisely to those within their own set:

> e.g. In initial sequences of voiceless consonants followed by voiced semi-vowels (= glides) the voicing of the semi-vowel may be slightly delayed by assimilation to the preceding voiceless consonant.

This is writing that is appropriate to the context; it is 'good' English only in so far as it communicates its meaning to its specialist audience. The writer did not intend that everyone should immediately understand everything he wrote. His vocabulary is appropriate to his subject matter and his audience which make up 'Context' just as well as English intended to make an immediate appeal to everyone: *Keep off the grass*; *Drinka Pinta Milka Day*; *No Entry*.

Structures

Two structures can be readily recognised in most writing:

Simple: the arrangement of simple statements beside each other. Often the statements are not joined by any conjunctions at all but are separated merely by full-stops or semi-colons; sometimes they are simply joined by *and, but, or,* or *either . . . or.*

Complex: the arrangement of statements so that they depend on each other. They are often joined by conjunctions such as: *because, although, if, unless, so that, until, on condition that.*

a) Children often use **simple** structures to narrate events.

> e.g. I got up and went downstairs. I had my breakfast and then had a wash. I got dressed and went to school. I was late and my teacher told me off.

Books of instruction and some scientific textbooks use structures like these in order to make the processes simple and clear.

e.g. Weigh a small test-tube. Introduce a small piece of marble and weigh again. Set up the apparatus. Weigh the whole apparatus. Then loosen the cork. The small tube will then slip down. etc.

> This is hardly elegant writing but it is clear and 'appropriate'. Sometimes, however, writers of literature deliberately choose simple structures to suggest strong emotions, drama, direct experience, or basic deeply-felt re-actions. For example, the following passage describes the experience of a short-sighted boy as he emerges from an optician's shop and sees the world clearly for the first time through his new pair of spectacles:

The lamplight! I looked in wonder at the diminishing crystals of gas-flames strung down the hill. Clapham was hung with necklaces of light, and the horses pulling the omnibuses struck the granite road with hooves of iron and ebony. I could see the skeletons inside the flesh and blood of the Saturday-night shoppers. The garments they wore were made of separate threads.

> This is writing that uses simple structures but it is clear, appropriate *and* elegant.

b) Nevertheless, writing which uses **complex** structures can be very effective indeed in conveying mood, altering pace, and producing an imaginative response from the reader. Take, for example, the following passage by the same writer who wrote about the boy with his new pair of spectacles (see above):

The lamp-lighter was a half-fairy figure, always followed by a number of children who danced about him and shouted with glee when he stopped at a lamp, flipped open a little glass trap-door at the bottom of the lantern, pushed his brass-topped pole into it, and kindled a fish-tail flame that flashed into life with a pop like a bursting balsam-seed.

> The choice of appropriate structures for your writing will allow you to indicate mood, vary pace, convey shades of meaning, change attitude, and regulate the responses of your readers. It is an art that will well repay the learning.

Punctuation

It is important to bear in mind that the way you punctuate your work will help the reader to understand what you are trying to say. If you use commas where full-stops are undeniably required the reader will be unable to follow your meaning; your ideas will run into each other and become garbled. This is perhaps the most common fault found in the work of unsuccessful candidates at examinations in English Language. It demonstrates very clearly that the writer has no conception of the structure of an English sentence and that he or she has scant regard for the reader.

There is an extreme view, sometimes held by lawyers, that if documents require punctuation to make their meaning clear then the expression of the law is unsound. Many insurance policies deliberately leave out all punctuation marks except capital letters; even these documents need to note where one statement ends and the next begins.

> e.g. No admission offer promise payment or indemnity shall be made or given by or on behalf of the insured without the written consent of the company which shall be entitled to take over and conduct in the name of the insured for its own benefit any claim and shall have full discretion in the conduct of any proceedings and in the settlement of any claim.

The relationship between writer and audience

6.3

The relationship and interaction between the writer or speaker and the audience are vital parts of the context in which language is used and it is here that the main differences between written and spoken English can be seen to come into play. These main differences arise particularly for the following reasons:

In written English

a) the person ('audience') for whom the writing is intended is not present and cannot respond to, and interact with, the writer;
b) the writer can plan ahead and can set his ideas down without interference or interruption from the 'audience';
c) the writer can have second thoughts and redraft his ideas to make them as effective as possible;
d) there are no distracting 'paralinguistic' features (such as gesture, tone, pitch, facial expression, etc.) to make the writer modify what he is saying.

The relationship between the user of the language (writer/speaker) and the person he or she is addressing (the 'audience') can range from the very close (father, mother, brother, sister, husband, wife) to the very distant and remote (judge, archbishop, king/queen). Between these two extremes lie relationships between boy-friend and girl-friend, pupil and teacher, patient and doctor, junior and senior colleagues, committee members and company chairman, etc.

Similarly, the use of language will be modified throughout this range from the intimate to the formal and explicit. The closer the relationship the less explicit the language needs to be: the more remote the relationship the more explicit the language will become.

In the context of a close relationship the language may be marked by short sentences, unfinished statements, imprecise vocabulary and (in speech) hesitation, pauses, space-fillers (er . . . um . . . d'you know . . . sort of . . .). Slang and colloquial expressions are often marked features of the language used in this context. An illustration of this kind of writing might be taken from the back of any picture postcard sent from one member of a family to another:

e.g. Arrived tired and hungry. Sea and weather gorgeous. Went for a walk along the cliffs this morning. Almost lost Harry over the edge. We're both fine. And you? Keep your pecker up! Love – Mabel and Harry.

In the context of a distant (remote) relationship the language will be marked by an absence of these more colloquial features and by more complex structures, precise vocabulary and (in speech) careful pronunciation. The comments of a barrister to a judge in the formal setting of a court of law will provide an example of such usage.

e.g. Your honour, may I draw your attention, with respect, to the defendant's insistence that he was elsewhere on the night of the alleged murder and that his plea of 'Not Guilty' rests firmly on the evidence to support his alibi?

Knowledge and experience held in common by the writer/speaker and the audience

6.4

This feature of the context in which language is used is also important, since it will have a modifying effect on the closeness or remoteness of the English used which has already been partly determined by the relationship between the writer/speaker and his or her audience. At this point the relationship and **the topic** of the writing or conversation will interact.

Boy-friend and girl-friend will have interests in common (e.g. music, clubs, sports, etc.) and they need not be explicit in their use of language.

e.g. 'You know that Eurythmics disc by Lennox Stewart – the
one we bought Saturday? I thought "You take some lentils . . .
and you take some rice" was better than the other side.'
'I liked "Who's that Girl?" It had a nice beat.'

A novelist or poet may well assume common experiences with his
reader – e.g. falling in love, greed, death, exhilaration – and need not
always be explicit in his or her descriptions. The experience, however,
may need to be heightened so that the audience is driven to see the
experience in a new light and so the language used by the writer must
convey by its very unusual quality the intenseness of the new view of
the experience. Take, for example, the opening lines of a poem by
Henry Vaughan (1622–95) in which he describes in a fresh and
startling way the common experience all human beings have at some
time or another of seeing beyond themselves to a new vision of life and
its ultimate reality:

I saw Eternity the other night
Like a great Ring of pure and endless light,
All calm as it was bright.

Or, Charles Dickens's description of the damp on a window early in
the morning:

I had seen the damp lying on the outside of my little window, as if
some goblin had been crying there all night, and using the
window for a pocket handkerchief.

(Great Expectations)

The writers assume the shared experience by heightening it for the
reader by their choice of language.

The knowledge skilled craftsmen or technicians have in common
also provides a context which conditions the language they use. They
readily fall back on **jargon**. (See above, p. 68.) Members of a trade or
profession – lawyers, doctors, teachers, carpenters – use a vocabulary
peculiar to their work almost as a kind of shorthand: It is far from being
careless, imprecise or slovenly; it is economical and accurate for their
work.

e.g. The muscles of the hand are subdivided into three groups: 1.
Those of the thumb, which occupy the radial side and produce
the thenar eminence; 2. Those of the little finger, which occupy
the ulnar side and give rise to the hypothenar eminence; 3. Those
in the middle of the palm and within the interosseous spaces.

Role-playing

6.5

A device frequently used in some English examinations or course-work exercises is that of asking the writer to 'Imagine that you are . . .' i.e. candidates are asked to adopt a role, a stance from which to write. During the course of a day, we all naturally play many roles – pupil, son or daughter, member of a gang, sulky individual, good neighbour, etc. – and so the device is not an unnatural one. The playing of a role, however, assumes a situation or a context in which to write or speak and this situation or context determines the kind of language we should use.

James Joyce's book *A Portrait of the Artist as a Young Man* sets out in biographical form the roles that Stephen Daedalus (or James Joyce himself) played from childhood to adolescence to young manhood. The author adopts the role of omniscient author but sets out to use language appropriate to each stage of the development of the boy; the role-playing is therefore reinforced by the language-use.

> e.g. Once upon a time and a very good time it was there was a moocow coming down along the road and this moocow that was coming down along the road met a nicens littles boy named baby tuckoo. . . .

The structures and the vocabulary, as well as the framework of a fairy story, mirror the stage of early childhood with which the first chapter of the book deals. The role-playing is carried into the language itself.

The difficulty in using language appropriate to a particular role is twofold: (a) that of choice of vocabulary and structures and (b) that of maintaining both the role and the level of language. When either or both of the difficulties assert themselves the user of the language becomes a figure of fun; such a figure is Dogberry in Shakespeare's *Much Ado about Nothing*.

The purpose(s) of writing or speaking

6.6

Another important feature of the context within which writing or speaking occurs is that of intention or purpose. *We write or speak with a purpose.* Examinations or course-work in English frequently present young people with a series of topics from which they are invited to choose one on which to write. The main purposes may be set out as follows:

a) to tell a story or narrate an incident (*narrative*);
b) to present or discuss an argument (*discursive*);
c) to set out facts (*exponential*);
d) to describe a scene or person or process (*descriptive*);
e) to persuade (*persuasive*);
f) to criticise (*critical*) in a humorous or scornful way (*satirical*);
g) to write from one's own experience (*subjective* or *personal*) or imagination (*creative*);
h) to develop a verbal exchange between characters (*dramatic*).

These 'kinds' of writing are considered in more detail in **Chapter 8** (pp. 106–23). The purpose for which the writing/speaking is intended, however, will condition the kind of language used and must be seen as a vital part of the context within which the writing/speaking is carried out.

The situation – time, place, atmosphere

6.7   It is self-evident that the language appropriate to a sermon is different in style from the language appropriate to a conversation on the terraces of a football stadium. The occasion is an important part of the context for language-use and the sensitive writer or speaker will never unintentionally make a mistake about it. If he or she *intentionally* creates a contrast in his style between language and occasion, then humour or parody will result. The person who speaks 'out of turn' with an unawareness of the situation, or of the time or place, is a stock figure of comedy and farce.

What is appropriate to the language of debate in the House of Commons with its formalities ('The Right Honourable Member' . . . 'Mr Speaker' . . .) will differ from the language of a brawl in the bar of a pub at closing time. Consider some of the possible contexts of situation time and place when each of the following might have been used:

a) Hop it!
b) How many more times do I have to tell you to clear off?
c) I think it's time you left.
d) May I ask you to take your company somewhere else?
e) Please leave now.
f) There is nothing further here for you.
g) Good night!

6.8   Although some of the elements within the context of language-use have been considered separately, it must be remembered that the notion of 'context' is complex and that these elements will interact readily one with the other. It is also essential to remember that a close interaction exists between writer/speaker, topic, context, and audience; all together will determine the kinds of language to be used, the level(s) of the language (register(s)), and the style.

Exercises

1 Write a letter to a person of the opposite sex who had shared an evening out with you at either a restaurant or a disco. The purpose of the letter is to express the pleasure you felt and to suggest gently that the relationship might continue. (Be careful about the 'register(s)' you decide to use.)

2   a) Continue the following narrative as an entry (about 150–200 words) in your personal diary:

    'I met a ghost tonight. . . .'

  b) Continue the following as the opening part (about 150–200 words) of an essay written by you for a formal, public examination:

    'Meeting a ghost can be a shattering experience. . . .'

  c) Continue the following as the opening part (about 150–200 words) of a talk about ghosts – given by you to a group of old-age pensioners at their weekly club meeting:

    'I met Flo last night. She used to live in Brixton, by the old Astoria – that is, until she passed on last year. Pneumonia it was. . . .'

3 Write a 'thank you' letter to a friend who had invited you for an evening to his or her flat and offered you a meal which you did not enjoy one bit. (Avoid making any statement which you know to be deliberately untrue.)

4 The following passage is part of a speech made by Winston Churchill in a broadcast to the French on 21 October 1940, shortly after the fall of France and during the Blitz by the German Luftwaffe on London. What features of it make it such a devastating attack on the Nazis and such an encouragement to the French (who still speak about it) at a time when they were smarting from their defeat and occupation?

    Frenchmen!
    For more than thirty years in peace and war I have marched

with you, and I am marching still along the same road. To-night I speak to you at your firesides wherever you may be, or whatever your fortunes are. I repeat the prayer around the louis d'or: 'Dieu protège la France'. Here at home in England, under the fire of the Boche, we do not forget the ties and links that unite us to France, and we are persevering steadfastly and in good heart in the cause of European freedom and fair dealing for the common people of all countries, for which, with you, we drew the sword. When good people get into trouble because they are attacked and heavily smitten by the vile and wicked, they must be very careful not to get at loggerheads with one another. The common enemy is always trying to bring this about, and, of course, in bad luck a lot of things happen which play into the enemy's hands. We must just make the best of things as they come along.

Here in London, which Herr Hitler says he will reduce to ashes, and which his aeroplanes are now bombarding, our people are bearing up unflinchingly. Our Air Force has more than held its own. We are waiting for the long-promised invasion. So are the fishes. But, of course, this for us is only the beginning. Now, in 1940, in spite of occasional losses, we have, as ever, command of the seas. In 1941 we shall have the command of the air. Remember what that means. Herr Hitler with his tanks and other mechanical weapons, and also by Fifth Column intrigue with traitors, has managed to subjugate for the time being most of the finest races in Europe, and his little Italian accomplice is trotting along hopefully and hungrily, but rather wearily and very timidly, at his side. They both wish to carve up France and her Empire as if it were a fowl: to one a leg, to another a wing or perhaps part of the breast. Not only the French Empire will be devoured by these two ugly customers, but Alsace-Lorraine will go once again under the German yoke, and Nice, Savoy, and Corsica – Napoleon's Corsica – will be torn from the fair realm of France. But Herr Hitler is not thinking only of stealing other people's territories, or flinging gobbets of them to his little confederate. I tell you truly what you must believe when I say that this evil man, this monstrous abortion of hatred and defeat, is resolved on nothing less than the complete wiping out of the French nation, and the disintegration of its whole life and future. By all kinds of sly and savage means he is plotting and working to quench for ever the fountain of characteristic French culture and of French inspiration to the world. All Europe, if he had his way, will be reduced to one uniform Boche-land, to be exploited, pillaged and bullied by his Nazi gangsters. You will excuse my speaking frankly, because this is not a time to mince words. It is not defeat that France will now be made to suffer at German hands, but the doom of complete obliteration. Army, Navy, Air Force, religion, law, language, culture, institutions, literature, history, tradition, all are to be effaced by the brute strength of a triumphant army and the scientific low-cunning of a ruthless Police Force.

Frenchmen – rearm your spirits before it is too late.

Goodnight then: sleep to gather strength for the morning. For the morning will come. Brightly will it shine on the brave and true, kindly upon all who suffer for the cause, glorious upon the tombs of heroes. Thus will shine the dawn. *Vive la France!* Long live also the forward march of the common people in all the lands towards their just and true inheritance, and towards the broader and fuller age.

(Winston Churchill, *The Second World War, vol 2*, Cassells, 1951, pp. 406–7.)

5   a) Read the following passage about a road accident from Richard Church's autobiography *Over the Bridge*. Examine it closely to see how it uses **simple** and **complex** constructions, dialogue, and reported speech to heighten the effect, control the pace and build to a climax. Notice, too, how 'the point of view' from which the event is narrated changes.

   b) Then, using some of the ways in writing you have noticed (and others, too, if you wish), give for a general reader you hope to interest an account of an accident (not necessarily a road accident) in which you have been involved:

We were bent over our handlebars, at the bottom of a sharp rise. Behind us rode a young man, alone, who had attached himself to us as we left Guildford, using us as pace-makers, perhaps. Jack was annoyed, for he hated collections of people, as being conspicuous demonstrations.

'Can't you let him go, Dad?' he said, urging Father to slow down. But Father had everything timed, and reduced to an economic output. His pace did not vary for some passing flipperdigibert of the road. He replied that we should be stopping soon for our midday meal, and that would enable us to shake off the stranger.

Suddenly we heard a cry of alarm. I raised my bemused head, and saw a stout woman on a tricycle, tearing down the hill with her feet off the pedals, which were flickering up and down, as it seemed, faster than the eye could follow. An instant later there was another cry from the stout woman, and a crash alongside us. The young man had pulled out, intending at last to pass our slow cortège. But he chose the wrong moment, for the tricyclist went slap into him. Machines and human bodies appeared immediately to multiply, and to be scattered all about us, amid a cloud of white dust, and groans and cries.

Jack and Father now both showed a common characteristic, for the bicycle with trailer, and the tandem, calmly slowed and stopped, the drivers dismounting and looking round in mild surprise. I had jumped clear, with a jolt that shook my bones, and I stood trembling, my eyes refusing, for a moment, to focus on the dreadful scene of carnage.

Father strode over to the mound of humanity in the middle of the road, lifted her up as though she were merely an inflated balloon, and assisted her to the side of the road.

'Now stay there!' he said, allowing her to relapse into tears and hysteria, while he returned to pick up the youth, who was kneeling within the frame of his bicycle, while the front wheel spun round, as an afterthought.

'Pull yourself together, lad!' cried Father. 'Your machine's not damaged. I've straightened the pedal, so you can push along before there are any questions asked. Wrong of you, y'know, turning out like that!'

His brusque warning acted like a pail of well water on the youth, who was obviously about to faint. Shaking himself, he stood up, took a deep breath, that brought the colour back to his hollow cheek.

'No fault of mine,' he muttered ungraciously, and stumbled off, walking his machine up the hill, examining it as he went.

Meanwhile Father was directing the tonic of his personality at the stout woman.

'Now, Ma'am!' he cried. 'Is nobody with you?'

By this time the poor husband approached down the hill on a bicycle of rare vintage, the back wheel being about two-thirds the size of the front one, and the chain encased in a honey-coloured, transparent gear-case square at both ends. The handlebars towered up, with grips of cork at least six inches long.

He was a small, nervous man, and he looked at my father beseechingly, like a spaniel.

'I will take charge,' he said. Though that was unbelievable, we left him and his runaway spouse, remounted and rode on.

6 Rewrite the account of the accident you gave in Exercise **5**, but this time reduce its length to give the bare facts as objectively as you can as if you are making a written statement as someone involved

in an accident to the police. (Before you begin, consider how this account will differ from your earlier description.)

7 Listen to a commentary on *either* a sporting event (e.g. a football match, a grand-prix race, a show-jumping competition) *or* a ceremonial occasion (e.g. the trooping of the colour, the opening of parliament) on *either* radio *or* television.

    a)   i)   How would the radio commentary have differed from that given on television?

           ii) What would be the factors accounting for the differences?

          iii) What features of the commentator's personality came across to his or her audience?

    b) Write the opening part of *either* a radio *or* a TV commentary (e.g. setting the scene and the start of the event) on *one* of the following:

        i)   a street demonstration;

        ii) a village fête;

        iii) a brass-band competition;

        iv) a gymnastic display.

8   a) Write a message to a close friend suitable for the back of a holiday postcard.

    b) Write the same message to the same friend as you might have presented it as a paragraph in a letter.

    c) Set down the fact that you wrote to a close friend and the details of what you wrote (in b) above) in the form of an entry in your own personal diary.

9   a) Write a letter to your best friend explaining why you have been unable to attend school or college recently. (He or she has been anxious about you.)

    b) Write a letter to the Head of your school or college explaining why you have been unable to attend recently. (He or she has telephoned your parents to know the reason.)

(*NB*. The purpose of this exercise is to give practice in the use of appropriate 'registers'; make sure you take account of this in the way you write the two letters.)

10 Write *two* sets of instructions how to carry out an operation which forms a central part of your main hobby (e.g. stripping an engine, opening a game of chess, adding to your collection of records, *etc*.):

    a) *first*, for someone who already knows a lot about your hobby;

    b) *secondly*, for someone who is about to take up the same hobby.

11 Give an account of the time you first fell in love for:

    a) a close friend with whom you share secrets; *and*

    b) a social worker who is trying to help you understand the problems of growing up.

12 Write a short paragraph, for inclusion in a novel you are writing, on each of the following common experiences in ways which make them new and fresh (see 6.4, pp. 00–00):

    a) the reflection of shop lights on a rainy pavement;

    b) being lost for words through a sudden shock;

    c) walking from a well-lit main road into a dark side-street;

    d) suddenly remembering an incident from childhood;

    e) the barking of a dog at day-break in the countryside.

13 Take the last piece of work you wrote for your teacher in school or college. Now imagine that you are an examiner reading it for assessment as part of an examination. Give an account of the thoughts which might run through your head as you play the role of 'examiner'.

14 The following is a fable by Æsop:

    a) rewrite the fable in a way that a very young child would understand it (say, a child of four or five); *and*

    b) Find a well-known fable for yourself and re-tell it in prose in a way which would interest an 18-year-old boy or girl:

An ass crossing a river with a load of salt lost his footing and slipped into the water so that the salt was dissolved. He was mightly pleased at finding himself relieved of his burden when he got upon his legs again. So the next time he came to a river with a load on his back, thinking that the same thing would happen if he got into the water, he let himself go under on purpose. But this time he was loaded with sponges, which absorbed so much water that he could not keep his head up and was drowned.

15 What do you think were the contexts of situation, place and/or time of the following? At whom were they directed? Try to give reasons for your judgements. (Check p. 159 for the origins of the comments.)

    a) I realise that patriotism is not enough. I must have no hatred or bitterness towards anyone.

    b) Make 'em laugh; make 'em cry, make 'em wait.

    c) Serve up in a clean dish, and throw the whole lot out of the window as fast as possible.

d) Sir, you have tasted two whole worms; you have hissed all my mystery lectures and been fighting a liar in the quad; you will leave Oxford by the next town drain.

e) Leaves with tooth-like lobes; outer flower bracts long, re-curved; heads large; fruit light brown. Very common in fields, lawns, waste places, by roadsides, etc. Flowers March–July.

f) If you cannot read a word:

    1. Pick out the sets of vowels.
    2. Divide into syllables.
    3. Sound each syllable.
    4. Put the syllables together.
    5. Play with the word.
    6. Read around the word.

g) She stepped out and I had to run her over before a stationary tree hit me.

h) When the red man signal shows, don't cross. Press the button on the box and wait. The lights will soon change and a steady green man signal will appear . . . After a short time the green man signal will begin to flash. This means that the lights will soon change again.

i) It is a truth universally acknowledged, that a single man in possession of a good fortune must be in want of a wife.

j) In accordance with your instructions I gave birth to twins on the form in the enclosed envelope.

7 The Audience

Writing and speaking are principally ways of communicating thoughts and feelings, hopes and experiences to other human beings. It is true that the very act of writing (or speaking) can be pleasurable in itself and allow us to express ideas and emotions and define our reactions to ourselves without any thought of an audience. Many write poetry for themselves: the soliloquy in drama (e.g. in *Hamlet*) is a conventionalised device which recognises that human beings do sometimes talk to themselves internally or aloud as a way of understanding and clarifying responses. Even here, however, a sense of 'audience' is implicit in the act of using language – the audience being one's own self.

7.1 Writing and speaking therefore presuppose that the language is directed at someone, who may or may not react and respond to what is written or said.

In situations using speech the persons talking change their roles from speaker to audience constantly and modify their language to take account of reactions and responses.

An understanding of 'audience' is essential to language activity and completes the complex pattern of *writer/speaker, topic* and *context* which all intereact to produce one form or style of language rather than another.

7.2 The relation between thought and language is crucial. Graham Wallas (1858–1932) wrote in his book *The Art of Thought*:

> The little girl had the makings of a poet in her who, being told to be sure of her meaning before she spoke, said: 'How can I know what I think till I see what I say?'

The quotation sets out one of the basic functions of languages – the precise formulation of ideas by using words; the words, in fact, become the idea or *are* the idea. This is not a new conception in philosophy – it was known to the Greeks and is at the heart of the meaning of the first verse of St John's Gospel:

> In the beginning was the Word, and the Word was with God, and the Word was God.

In an admirable book *Clear Thinking*, (first published in 1936), R. W. Jepson summarised the point:

Until a thought is translated into language, it remains vague, nebulous and indeterminate: language crystallises it and gives it form and substance . . . the very process of having to put our thoughts into speech or writing, and the effort entailed in discovering adequate expression for them, are of themselves thought-clarifiers.

Self as the audience

7.3

Quite often students use this form of writing for themselves when they are making notes in class or from textbooks. To be of use such notes need to be brief and clear. The art of note-making is well worth acquiring.

The 'self' acts as the audience, too, for some forms of writing such as entries in personal diaries, which are intended to be read by no one but the writer.

Diary entries were fully discussed in **Chapter 2** (pp. 20–2) where it was pointed out that in a personal diary published after the writer's tragic death, a teenage girl, Anne Frank, gave her other self whom she addressed directly a name of her own – Kitty. Such entries are intimate and self-revealing and the language used can be idiosyncratic to the point where normal sentence-structures are abandoned and new vocabulary is invented and introduced.

A named person as the audience

7.4

This might be a friend, a close relative, or a well-known public figure.

Many exercises in school or college ask for personal letters to be written to someone whom the student knows well. They are attempts to encourage good personal writing and are closest, perhaps, to real-life situations which the writer experiences; he or she does not have to play a role since letter-writing to friends or close relatives is a normal activity and forms one of the actual situations where writing has a practical purpose. After formal education has finished, few will need to write essays or plays, but all will need to write to friends, relatives, trade or business personnel, colleagues or acquaintances at some time.

The writing where the audience is specifically named can be intensely personal. It will take account of:

a) the character of the writer and his or her special interests, attitudes, and activities;
b) the character of the named person and his or her special interests, attitudes, and activities;
c) the nature of the relationship between the writer and the named person.

Clearly, assumptions can be made by the writer about shared interests, knowledge, and activities and he or she can draw upon remembered incidents and feelings which both writer and audience experienced together. The style can be as intensely personal and intimate as the writer wishes. Similarly, in talking to a close friend or relative, pauses need not be awkward; interruptions and changes in topic occur naturally and easily and the conversation becomes a shared experience rather than an occasion to impress, explain, or dominate. There is an atmosphere of relaxed, shared dialogue implicit in the writing or speaking when a close, named person is the 'audience'.

Where the named person is more remote, perhaps a public figure or the manager of a company or the head teacher, the writing or speaking will need to take special account of the relationship between the writer and the audience. Again, the style will need to be adapted by both topic and context as well as by this relationship.

An unnamed person as the audience

7.5

It is here, for instance in writing to an unknown faceless official, that many people have the greatest difficulty in finding an appropriate level of English and an appropriate style to use. The language can become very stilted and even impossible to understand.

Consider the following extracts from letters written to an unknown official in a Social Security office in the north; they all try to make a point but how far is the level of English appropriate to the situation and purpose?

a)

> I can't go out to work as I'm tied up at home. Every time I try to get a job my old mother stops me. I can't leave the house. She is unable to move and has not been out shopping for the last ten years. Can you help me? Someone told me I need an attendance allowance but I need more than that. I need some form of medical help.

b)

> Will you please send me all the information you have about the national Health? My own doctor needs changing and I don't know how to do it. Is there a form or something? He has not been well himself lately and its off colour. As a result he cannot come out late at night when I call him but sends a loco round instead.

c)

> With regard to your recent correspondence to hand, I am writing to say I have seven children and have lost two others. Please tell me what I ought to do about it. I am desperate and cannot be held responsible for my actions. The last two social workers I have had told me not to worry but it is all right for them. They are not married.

d)

> I enclose form 95DXN. You will see I didn't know how to fill it in, especially the bit asking where I live. I don't live anywhere but I'm squatting at the moment. It can't go on much longer. Can you accommodate me? You must have a flat somewhere. What about one of those houses built on purpose in Artillery Street?

Part of the problem of writing faced by these letter-writers which led them into making such hilarious statements was that they felt they were writing to an office, or a post, or a 'disembodied' official rather than to a fellow human being. They had preconceived notions about those working on the other side of a desk, their role, and their attitudes; they also felt that a certain style was necessary to write to such officials but they were none too sure of how to control it. A stereotyped 'audience' seemed to call for a 'stereotyped' style of writing.

An unknown general audience

7.6

The most difficult writing of all is that where the audience is unknown, since the writer has to adopt a role which may be generalised to the point where he or she no longer recognises himself or herself. If assumptions about interests and experiences in common have to be made, then the direction of the writing inevitably becomes imprecise. The fact is that in real-life situations where talking and writing are important activities we never have to talk or write without knowing at which 'audience' the language is directed. Even 'the general reader' may be specific enough to allow a writer or speaker to find his or her bearings.

In such situations where the audience is totally unspecified, the writer has to:

a) adopt a specific point of view about himself or herself and maintain it;
b) make assumptions about the topic's relevance to most other people;
c) invent an audience such as 'the general reader', or 'Everyman', or some specific person for whom the writing can be defined;
d) care deeply about the validity of what he is writing or saying and be committed to it;
e) recognise that what is being written or said will need some modification and qualification.

Many topics set for examinations or course-work exercises do not specify an audience, unfortunately. The candidate is therefore forced to establish these five areas as clearly as possible in relation to the topics before beginning to write. Let us take, for example, the topic 'Ghosts'. The treatment is left entirely to the candidate; the opening should establish viewpoint, attitude to the topic, context, and audience – all of the candidate's own choosing. Consider the following as possible openings to a composition or piece of writing on the topic:

a) Dear Ghost,
   Thank you for your visit again last night. I found it the most terrifying yet; you are obviously getting the knack of haunting now. . . .
b) My grandfather is a ghost – not a particularly obvious one, but he does turn up on the oddest occasions. The first time he 'manifested' himself (I think that is the right word) was when. . . .
c) Do I believe in ghosts? Yes, I suppose I do. After all, it is hard to accept that the thinking, feeling part of me just stops dead one day. Let me give you my reasons for believing in ghosts. . . .

d) Ghosts are the wild creations of a disordered imagination. Many claim to have seen ghosts or to have had occult experiences but the evidence of such visits remains insubstantial and unproved. From a scientific point of view to postulate the existence of ghosts would be unacceptable. . . .

e) *October 31.* Halloween. I saw her again. Crinoline, low-cut bodice, large low-brimmed hat. This time she smiled. Still beckoning me away with that raised, delicate finger. Vanished gradually.
November 1. All Saints Day. She spoke – not in English. I am going mad, I think. . . .

The teacher or examiner as audience

A distinction needs to be made between writing for a teacher and writing for an examiner, a distinction that rests on the distancing of the writing from the writer to the reader.

Students at school or in college often write to produce a response in a particular teacher; much depends, therefore, on their relationship and the confidence that exists between them. Some write for what they consider is the stereotyped response of a teacher without having a particular teacher in mind; others write for a teacher who is liked or disliked, respected or not respected. In other words, the writing assumes a form likely to evoke a considered response: 'He'll like that' or 'That's the way she told us to do it' or 'She won't be expecting that from me'.

Writing for an examiner is often surprisingly frank and uninhibited; the distance between the candidate and the assessor is great enough for judgements to be without recrimination, perhaps. Confessions, attempts to shock, subservience to preconceived notions of what examiners are, all feature in the writing of candidates. It is as well to remember, however, that examiners are real human beings with sensitivities, prejudices, experiences every bit as real as the candidate's own.

7.7

The peer group as audience

Curiously, young people find writing for their peers difficult. The problem lies partly in the fact that their own adoption of a particular role as writer is likely to come under criticism from other members of

7.8

the group and partly because few are willing to expose themselves on a particular topic to what is likely to be a deflating and highly critical audience.

Writing for a school magazine or broadsheet often reveals much of the embarrassment of writing for a peer group. Often young people try to escape from the predicament by implicitly substituting the teacher as audience for the peer group or by imitating the style of other writers (such as those working for sports magazines, newspapers, or novelists who are directing their writing at quite another kind of reader) or even by cracking in-jokes.

Consider the main features of the following extracts from school magazines. What 'awkwardness' can you detect in the writing for a peer group? What implicit imitation of other styles can you see? How uneasy is the stance of the writer?

a) Apart from a short break at the end of last term, when the key to the chess club cupboard was lost, the club has met regularly as usual. I think the chess club can claim to meet more frequently than any other School society.

   As Easter is approached and passed each year, the chess season bursts out into a blaze of glory and then fades away as serious chess is forgotten until next winter. We are an exception because the House Championships have not even started by Easter. Did I say 'serious chess' . . .?

b) Apologies for any defects of typing or presentation. Problems of producing this magazine are far greater than any met in Fleet Street – such as one's entire fleet (*sic*) of typists having finished courses and left on holiday six weeks ago, and one's artist-in-chief having to go home half way through designing a front cover. (Due to this cover crisis, thanks are due, believe it or not, to the editor's sister, who insists on being mentioned, for her help. While I'm about it, Hallo Mum.)

c) We were all rather tired that night and fell asleep quite quickly. In the middle of the night we were all suddenly woken up by a raging fight which was ensuing between Peter and a local moth.

   On average we had all taken about thirty pounds each for the holiday and already half of it had gone. We therefore decided to economise on lunches.

   The youth hostel was modernly equipped and run by two very helpful old women. Whilst we were there the local band came back from Holland. Most of them were completely drunk and their recital ended in utter chaos.

The specified type as audience

It is helpful for good writing to have a specified type of reader as an 'audience'. It provides an objective at which to direct and project ideas. Consider the following topics where an attempt is made to specify a type of reader.

7.9

a) *Either:* Explain the interest in stamp-collecting *to someone who thinks it is a boring hobby;*
   Or: Justify your enthusiasm for collecting British stamps *to another philatelist whose interest lies in foreign stamps.*
b) Describe how to ride a powerful motorcycle *to:*
   i) *someone who has experience only of riding bicycles;*
   ii) *someone who has never seen a motorcycle before.*
c) *Either:* Explain *to a teenager who uses make-up too heavily* the fundamental principles of applying make-up effectively;
   Or: Present an argument for girls using make-up *to a teenage boy who thinks it is silly.*

The '**audience**' will determine, along with the **writer's viewpoint**, the **topic**, and the **context**, the level of language and the style to be used by a writer or speaker. Both must be appropriate to **all four elements** that go to make up the writing or speaking activity.

7.10

Exercises

1 What topic would writers be dealing with if they used the following sets of words of phrases? With the help of a dictionary explain what the words mean in the context of the topic.

   a) First-day issue; perforation; overprint;
   b) tack; snaffle; crupper;
   c) pointillism; impressionist; perspective;
   d) two-stroke; big-end; exhaust valve;
   e) terminals; print wheel; megabytes;
   f) equilateral; scalene; isosceles;
   g) character; conflict; denouement;
   h) gambit; mate; castle;
   i) turbo-charged; grid; pole-position;
   j) colander; bain-marie; fish-kettle.

2 Find as many words of similar meaning (synonyms) as you can for each of the following:

> e.g. *calm:* cool, composed, serene, unruffled, undisturbed

> a) *change;* b) *courage;* c) *dark;* d) *error;* e) *feeling;* f) *hinder;* g) *know;* h) *move;* i) *power;* j) *ugly.*

(Notice how the words you choose differ very slightly in their meaning; used within the context of a sentence the words would take on a sharper definition.)

3 Keep a personal diary for one week. Include in it, day by day, not only a brief account of what you do but also some of your thoughts, observations, and feelings. (Read 7.3, p. 97, carefully before you begin.)

4 Read 7.4, pp. 97–8, carefully and then write to a friend or a close relative, a personal letter which includes *one* of the following topics as a major part of its contents:

> a) an account of a new bicycle you have just bought;
> b) a visit you made recently to a mutual acquaintance;
> c) your response to his or her request for a loan of £100;
> d) an acceptance of the offer to share a continental holiday;
> e) your refusal to join in a dangerous (and illegal) adventure.

5 Imagine that you left school or college three years ago and now require an open testimonial from your former head teacher or principal. Write a letter asking for such a testimonial and bringing him or her up to date with your activities since leaving.

6 Write an official letter to an unknown manager of your local Department of Employment office explaining that you have recently become unemployed and need help in securing benefits due to you and in finding a new job. (Read 7.5, pp. 88–9, carefully before you begin.)

7 Read 7.6, pp. 100–1, and then write for an unspecified general reader five possible openings to a composition on *one* of the following topics:

> a) Things that go bump in the night.
> b) The local policeman.
> c) Race-relations.
> d) Your favourite foods.
> e) Comprehensive schools.

8 Read 7.7, p. 106, and then write two openings of compositions, one directed towards your teacher as reader and one

directed towards an unknown examiner, for each of the following topics:
  a) My school (or college) as I see it.
  b) Teachers I have known.

9 Write an account for your school (or college) newspaper or magazine of the first time you visited *either* your boy-friend's (or girl-friend's) home *or* a 'Top-of-the-Pops' TV recording session for the first time. Your writing should be directed towards those in the same year-groups as yourself.

10 Write about 300 words on *one* of the following:

  a) a defence of the latest teenage fashion in hair styles to a relative of your parents' generation;
  b) a reply to a newspaper article which tried to justify an increase in the nation's armaments;
  c) an attack on (or a defence of) a newspaper feature-writer who has proposed the abolition of all dogs as pets on the grounds of hygiene.

8 Kinds of Writing

Once the **writer's point of view**, the **topic**, the **context**, and the **audience** have been defined as far as possible, it does not necessarily mean that only one variety or kind of English remains open. The writer is not the linguistic prisoner of a defined situation; he or she remains free to make choices from the wide variety of styles and linguistic skills within his or her powers. Good writing (or speaking) will often combine styles or move easily from one kind to another.

In **Chapter 6** (pp. 80–9) the following categories of writing were identified; the categories were not considered necessarily discrete:

narrative; discursive; exponential; descriptive; persuasive; critical (satirical); personal (creative); dramatic.

Narrative writing

8.1

The order in which the events in a narrative occur is of considerable importance. The writing needs to start relevantly and to engage the reader's attention at once. Too often long accounts of day breaking, the weather, and getting up impede the impact of a narrative's opening; go quickly and centrally into the topic.

The maxim that 'a story should have a beginning, a middle, and an end' is sound, but the arrangements of the events need not demand that their order should be chronological. Some very famous stories begin with the middle or end of the series of events and the beginning is arrived at by means of a 'flashback'.

In the course of the writing it is helpful if the pace is varied: some exciting/dramatic moments or turns in the story may be followed by periods when the tension is deliberately lowered. Action, description, and comment should be used to support each other. The ending of a narrative should clearly resolve the events or at least point to some further problems, as in some ghost stories, where the reader may need to continue to think and seek answers to questions.

Some beginnings

a) Three hundred miles and more from Chimborazo, one hundred from the snows of Cotopaxi, in the wildest wastes of Equador's Andes, there lies that mysterious mountain valley, cut off from the world of men, the Country of the Blind.

(Notice the immediate entry into the main topic, the building-up of a fairy-tale atmosphere by means of musical, far-off names, and the insistence that the story must be taken on its own terms with the disbelief of the reader willingly suspended.)

b) It was Joe Dillon who introduced the Wild West to us. He had a little library made up of old numbers of *The Union Jack*, *Pluck*, and *The Halfpenny Marvel*. Every evening after school we met in his back garden and arranged Indian battles . . .

(Notice the swift opening, the introduction of the writer's standpoint, the atmosphere of childhood imaginativeness, the selection of details and the immediate arrival of the main topics — confrontation and innocence.)

c) 'How are your funny friends at Potter's Farm, Johnnie?' asked his aunt from London.
 'Very well, thank you, Aunt Eva,' said the little boy in the window in a high prim voice. He had been drawing faces on his bare knee and now put down the indelible pencil. The moment that he had been dreading all day had arrived. Now they would probe and probe with their silly questions and the whole story of that dreadful tea party with his old friends would come tumbling out.

(This becomes a horrific story of two elderly sisters who mutilate a bird in front of a sensitive boy. The story begins quietly by distancing the child from the adults around him, as they intrude on his imagination; it continues from the viewpoint of the omniscient author but enters into childhood's fantasies and confrontations with reality in a shattering way. Notice, particularly, the very effective way of introducing narrative with a snatch of dialogue.)

Some endings

a) Two in the morning, he says, is the time she (the Dream Woman) will find him, one of these days. Two in the morning is the time, all the year round, when he likes to be most certain that he has got the clasp knife safe about him. He does not mind being alone, as long as he is awake, except on the night before his birthday, when he firmly believes himself to be in peril of his life. The birthday has only come round once since he has been here, and then he sat up along with the night-porter. 'She's looking for me,' is all he says, when anybody speaks to him about the one anxiety of his life; 'she's looking for me.' He might be right. She *may* be looking for him. 'Who can tell? Who can tell?' said I.

(Notice the way the horror of this ghost story is deliberately left unresolved as the nightmarish events revert back to reality and to the narrator. The repeated question bodes evil.)

b) (In *Mr Loveday's Little Outing* by Evelyn Waugh, a gentle, elderly man, Mr Loveday has been locked up in a mental asylum for thirty-five years for strangling a young girl cyclist. Angela Moping, an upper-class young lady bent on doing good at all costs, secures Loveday's release by pleading his case with officials. Two hours after being released, Loveday returns to the asylum unexpectedly and the story resolves itself dramatically by means of dialogue and narrative. The irony in the words and the context of the story add its own moment of horror to the ending.)

'I have come back,' he informed the doctor. 'I think that now I shall be here for good.'
'But, Loveday, what a short holiday. I'm afraid that you have hardly enjoyed yourself at all.'
'Oh yes, sir, thank you, sir, I've enjoyed myself *very much*. I'd been promising myself one little treat, all these years. It was short, sir, but *most* enjoyable. Now I shall be able to settle down to my work here without any regrets.'
Half a mile up the road from the asylum gates, they later discovered an abandoned bicycle. It was a lady's machine of some antiquity. Quite near it in the ditch lay the strangled body of a young woman, who, riding home to her tea, had chanced to overtake Mr Loveday, as he strode along, musing on his opportunities.

c) (At the end of his brilliant science fiction short story, *The Sentinel*, Arthur C. Clarke warns that man has reached the point where he is faced with the consequences of his own scientific skills and has to make a choice between life and death. Man needs help and may have to find it from worlds outside his own. The story concludes on a thoughtful note written from the personal viewpoint of the writer.)

I can never look now at the Milky Way without wondering from which of those banked clouds of stars the emissaries are coming. If you will pardon so commonplace a simile, we have broken the glass of the fire-alarm and have nothing to do but to wait.

I do not think we will have to wait for long.

d) Consider now a complete short story written by a 13-year-old boy. The writer's point of view, the topic, the context, and the audience are all soundly established. The narrative has a beginning, a middle and an end; there are some interesting 'twists' to the story; details are carefully selected; there is a delightful surprise in the ending. The topic set was 'The Empty House', a familiar enough subject but here given very unfamiliar treatment.

WITHOUT THE GHOST OF A SMILE

It was something he said, and then in cold realism I knew I was talking to a ghost.

And well I remember it. It was about five years ago. I was enjoying the welcome quiet of an empty house and settled down to reading with enthusiasm. The book had been recommended to me by a friend whose personal knowledge of the author ensured I would be gripped by it.

My surroundings faded as I got deeper into the story and the characters seemed to come alive. Then I had a strange sensation that I was no longer alone in the room. I broke from the grip of the book and looked around me but I could see no-one. Surely that was a human voice I heard?

'Who's there?' I called, irritated at the thought of being interrupted from my story. Then it struck me – I was alone in the house. I repeated my call a little less confidently.

'Who's there?'

I wondered momentarily if my friend was playing a rather feeble joke but dismissed the thought when I remembered he was abroad.

The sound came again but this time it was more distinguishable.

'Help! Please help me!'

The words rang in my ears; beads of sweat broke out upon my forehead; my eyes peered intently but I could see nothing.

'How can I help you? What do you want me to do?' The words tumbled forth from my mouth, without my being aware of having spoken. All I got for an answer was the cry repeated.

'Who are you? What do you want of me?' I said, paralysed with fear by this time.

Then I felt its presence even nearer.

'Give it to him,' the voice muttered.

'Give what?' I asked, but I had no need to as I already had a sheet of paper in my hand.

'But to whom must I give it? and why?'

'Please I must get it quickly,' the voice continued as if I had not spoken.

'He must be stopped from going or his life is forfeit.'

'Who? What is the danger? Please, you must give me more information.'

'If he does not receive it he will be dead within the hour,' the voice went on unheedingly. 'In fact it may even now be too late.' The voice seemed fainter. 'Please try to reach him in time. He must get it. Please . . .'

The room suddenly seemed overpowering; my instincts urged me to get out as soon as I could. I reached the door but it was shut tight. Somehow the lock had jammed. It was too strong a door for me to break through. I began to panic. I looked around the room hastily. The window! I should be able to get through that. It opened noiselessly and without any trouble. I looked out. There was soft ground below. I should be able to drop to the ground comfortably. I straddled the window-ledge with my left leg on the outside when something took hold of my right leg and pulled, and pulled, and kept pulling my leg – as I have been pulling yours.

Discursive (discussion) writing

8.2 The essential factors in writing a piece which discusses a topic are *selection* and *order*.

What is included in an argument and what is omitted will help to condition its success. Moreover, decisions have to be made about which points should be developed and well illustrated and which points played down. A leading article in *The Times, The Daily Telegraph,* or *The Guardian* will amply illustrate the ways in which selection and emphasis work in the presentation of a view – but again the **point of view** from which the article is written, the **topic** itself, the **context** (political, economic, social) at the moment, and the **readership** at which it is directed will all condition the kind of language and the style of what actually appears.

The order in which the facts are presented is also important. A simple structure, such as 'Pros' followed by 'Cons' *or* Firstly . . . Secondly . . . Thirdly . . . Finally, can be effective. Paragraphing is of crucial significance in discursive writing, since it marks the stages of the argument and helps to provide balance and contrast.

In an article aimed at teachers in Colleges of Further Education and intended to criticise them for not showing initiative, a leader writer in *The Times Educational Supplement* selected and ordered his comments very effectively in the following passage. Notice how the relaxed style and easy level of vocabulary as well as the use of rhetorical questions all serve to emphasise his point and make the Further Education lecturers who missed an opportunity, at a time when it was vital for their continued prosperity to provide new courses, squirm.

ON WITH THE DANCE

The cult of aerobics has proved a money-spinner for those who saw that keep fit combined with rock music and Miss Jane Fonda was just what the affluent society was waiting for. Unfortunately, too many of the instructors who take aerobic classes are unqualified and may be dangerous. An excessive dose of physical jerks, with or without the thump of rock music, can lead to sprains and strains and stress fractures of the kind suffered by over-trained athletes.

So what? A craze for over-fed, guilt-ridden, town-dwellers earnestly kidding themselves that by pushing themselves to the limit they can satisfy their fantasies? Partly this, and partly just the irresponsible rag, tag and bobtail, trailed by the main body of aerobic classes, which provide enjoyable and healthy exercise in pleasant surroundings for those who can afford to pay high fees.

There seems an obvious case for some regulation of standards of instruction and accreditation of instructors. But such regulations should be the least necessary to protect the public. The new money-spinners spotted a social need which adult education failed to recognise. They exploited it by aggressive marketing and proved a case for free enterprise in fitness. Good luck to them. But why did the FE colleges let them get away with it?

Exponential writing

8.3

Some of the ways in which facts are set out from an objective point of view were fully discussed in **Chapter 4** (pp. 51–61). However, frequently the need arises to set out facts or to outline the stages in a process where the third person (he/she/they; him/her/them) is not the best way to present facts. Consider some of the following ways as alternatives. What advantages do they have in making an impact on the audience?

a) The use of tables

e.g. A table setting out how much homework time for a sample of 939 pupils during a given week was spent on different writing activities as part of the English course:

Homework	Minutes: 0	1–30	31–60	61–90	91–120	121–150	Over 150
i stories and plays	698	176	62	1	2	—	—
ii from personal experience	747	156	33	3	—	—	—
iii argument and exposition	860	69	10	—	—	—	—
iv description	793	126	19	1	—	—	—
v reproductive, i.e. writing in pupil's own words of material derived from printed or oral sources	777	134	26	1	—	1	—
vi letters	901	35	3	—	—	—	—
vii verse	866	66	7	—	—	—	—
vii copying of existing printed material, e.g. for anthologies or topics	903	31	5	—	—	—	—
ix written corrections and fair copying of own work	823	112	4	—	—	—	—

b) The use of displayed material (especially in advertisements)

e.g.

c) The use of maps and diagrams

e.g. The conquest of southern England by the Normans following the Battle of Hastings in 1066.

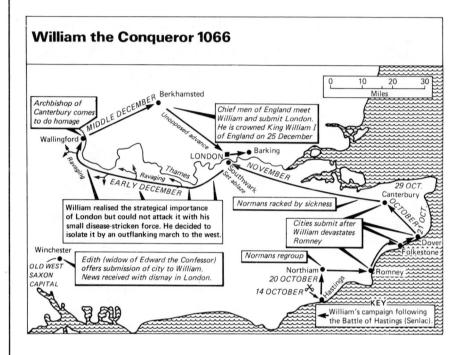

William the Conqueror 1066

Archbishop of Canterbury comes to do homage

MIDDLE DECEMBER   Berkhamsted

Unopposed advance

Chief men of England meet William and submit London. He is crowned King William I of England on 25 December

Wallingford

Ravaging

Thames

LONDON   ● Barking

Ravaging   Southwark Set ablaze

EARLY DECEMBER

NOVEMBER

29 OCT. Canterbury

William realised the strategical importance of London but could not attack it with his small disease-stricken force. He decided to isolate it by an outflanking march to the west.

Normans racked by sickness

OCTOBER   27 OCT

Cities submit after William devastates Romney

Winchester

OLD WEST SAXON CAPITAL

Edith (widow of Edward the Confessor) offers submission of city to William. News received with dismay in London.

Dover
Folkestone

Normans regroup

Northiam ●
20 OCTOBER

14 OCTOBER   Hastings

Romney

KEY
William's campaign following the Battle of Hastings (Senlac).

0   10   20   30
Miles

d) The use of graphs

Methods of grouping pupils for the teaching of 12 and 14-year-old children in English classes.

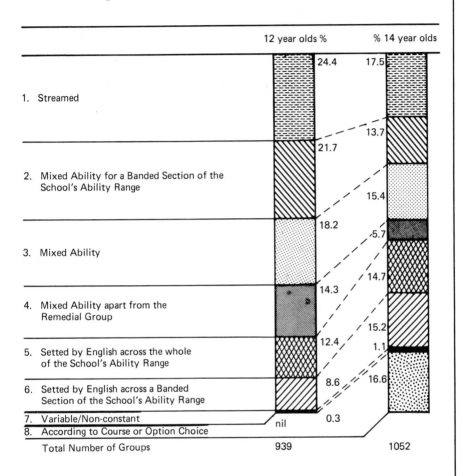

	12 year olds %	% 14 year olds
1. Streamed	24.4	17.5
2. Mixed Ability for a Banded Section of the School's Ability Range	21.7	13.7
3. Mixed Ability	18.2	15.4
4. Mixed Ability apart from the Remedial Group	14.3	5.7
5. Setted by English across the whole of the School's Ability Range	12.4	14.7
6. Setted by English across a Banded Section of the School's Ability Range	8.6	15.2
7. Variable/Non-constant	nil	1.1
8. According to Course or Option Choice		16.6
		0.3
Total Number of Groups	939	1052

e) The use of diagrams accompanied by explanations

e.g. A vacuum flask

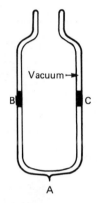

Sir James Dewar (1892) invented the vacuum flask for storing-liquid air. The temperature of this is 180° below freezing-point on the Centigrade scale (*i.e.* −180° C.), so that if it were kept in an ordinary vessel, heat would quickly reach it from the surroundings and it would vaporise. Nowadays vacuum flasks are extensively used for holding liquids which we want to keep hot. The flask consists of a double-walled vessel of thin glass (see fig.). The air is pumped out from between the walls through a tube at A, which is afterwards sealed up. The inside of the outer wall and the outside of the inner wall are silvered. B and C are small pads of felt to prevent the glass breaking because of vibration.

When a hot liquid is put into the flask heat cannot easily escape from the inner wall to the outer, because the silver surface of this inner wall is a bad radiator and there is no air to enable convection currents to be set up. There is little conduction through the thin glass, because it is a bad conductor, whilst most of the heat radiated is reflected back from the silvered surface, which is a bad absorber. If the cork were not put in, convection currents would be set up and the contents would cool, but the cork limits the convection currents to the small air space above the liquid.

f) Instructions

(e.g. recipes, car workshop manuals, directions for use on the packaging of products, etc.)

This is a very common form of 'exponential' writing. Normally the topic, the context, and the audience are very specific. The writer adopts the viewpoint of the instructor and arranges his or her facts in a clear and ordered way; the sentences are usually short and the verbs (the key words in sentences) are usually in the imperative (commanding) mood.

e.g.

SHEEP'S HEAD

A sheep's head
Bouquet garni
10 peppercorns

Salt and pepper
2 tablesp. pearl barley
or rice

2 onions	1 oz. butter *or* fat
1 small turnip	1 oz. flour
2 small carrots	Parsley

If necessary, split the head and remove the brains. Wash the head several times, taking care to remove all splintered bones. Scrape the small bones from the nostrils and brush the teeth. Soak in salt water for 30 min. Cover with cold water and bring to the boil. Pour away the water and replace with fresh cold water and add the bouquet garni, peppercorns and salt. Boil up and skim well. Add the barley (blanched) or rice. Cook slowly for about 3 hr. Meanwhile prepare the vegetables and cut into dice; these should be added about 1 hr. before serving. Remove the skin and fibres from the brains with salt and wash in cold water. Tie the brains in muslin and cook with the head for about 15–20 min. Then chop coarsely. Heat the fat in a saucepan and add the flour. Stir over the heat and cook without browning for about 3 min., then add ¾pt. of liquid in which the head is cooking. Stir until boiling, correct the seasoning and add the brains. Remove the head and take all the flesh from the bones. Skin and slice the tongue. Place the meat neatly on a hot dish. Pour the brain sauce over. If liked, garnish with some of the sliced tongue, vegetables and chopped parsley. Serve the broth separately.
3 helpings.

Descriptive writing

Good descriptive writing demands control – control of pace, mood and the patterning of language – and a clear point of view. Detail, sharp observation, and relevant comparisons mark effective descriptive writing. Consider the following descriptions of a) a person, b) a place, and c) a process to see if you can isolate the important stylistic features of each:

8.4

a) A person

A fearful man, all in coarse grey, with a great iron on his leg. A man with no hat, and with broken shoes, and with an old rag tied round his head. A man who had been soaked in water, and smothered in mud, and lamed by stones, and cut by flints, and stung by nettles, and torn by briars; who limped and shivered, and glared and growled; and whose teeth chattered in his head as he seized me by the chin.

b) A place

In the centre of the village, near the Hamlet School, a narrow triangle of ground hemmed in by the High Street and Court Lane, stood a Huguenot cemetery, its headstones and monuments awry, many of them yawning to show rough brickwork beneath the sculptured stone. Trees towered over the neglected tombs, and the annual tides of grasses and wild flowers rose above them, broke in sprays of seeds and ebbed again. It was enclosed by locked gates of hand-wrought iron, over-arched by an empty lamp-cage.

c) A process

A particularly benighted landsman must imagine the act of anchoring as a process of throwing something overboard, where-as the anchor ready for its work is already overboard, and is not thrown over, but simply allowed to fall. It hangs from the ship's side at the end of a heavy, projecting timber called the cat-head, in the bight* of a short, thick chain whose end link is suddenly released by a blow from a top-maul or the pull of a lever when the order 'Let go!' is given.

* coil

Persuasive writing

8.5

It is here that the writer's point of view, the topic, the context, and the direction of the writing need to be in very close harmony. There is no single formula to produce effective writing which persuades a reader to accept an argument, change his or her mind, buy a product, or to apply for a new post, etc.

Some writers prefer a direct, frontal attack on the reader, exploiting his hopes or his doubts and fears. Charles Haddan Spurgeon was a popular preacher in the middle of the nineteenth century. His sermons read a little oddly today, but they still burn with a passionate intensity because of the directness of their language:

I do not think that one of the worst sins a man can be guilty of in this world is to be idle. I can almost forgive a drunkard, but a lazy man there is very little pardon for. The most abominable thing in the world is for a man to let the grass grow up to his ankles and do nothing. God never sent a man into the world to be idle. But there are some who make a tolerably fair profession and who do nothing from one year's end to the other.

Often, however, the writing or the speaking becomes effective because of its deliberate understatement *or* its irony. One of the most moving appeals to stir the hearts of an audience occurred in the reply of a Red Indian Chief, Seattle, in 1854 to the American white men who were about to take the Indians' tribal lands and put them into reservations. The poignancy and the appeal of the repeated phrases and the contrasting descriptions account partly for its persuasiveness. What else can you find to account for its powerful effect?

> The sight of your cities pains the eyes of the red man. But perhaps it is because the red man is a savage and does not understand.
>
> There is no quiet place in the white man's cities. No place to hear the unfurling of leaves in spring, or the rustle of insects' wings. But perhaps it is because I am a savage and do not understand. The clatter only seems to insult the ears. And what is there to life if a man cannot hear the lonely cry of the whippoorwill or the arguments of the frogs around a pond at night? I am a red man and do not understand. The Indian prefers the soft sound of the wind darting over the face of a pond, and the smell of the wind itself, cleansed by a midday rain or scented with the pinon pine.
>
> But if we sell you our land, you must remember that the air is precious to us, that the air shares its spirit with all the life it supports. And if we sell you our land, you must keep it apart and sacred, as a place where even the white man can go to taste the wind that is sweetened by the meadow's flowers.
>
> One thing we know, Our God is the same God. This earth is precious to him. Even the white man cannot be exempt from the common destiny. We may be brothers after all. We shall see.

The plea failed because the Indian chief failed to estimate correctly the sensitivity (or insensitivity) of his audience.

Critical writing

A piece of writing which sets out to be critical must take careful note of the audience at which it is being directed. Once this has been established and the purpose of the writing clarified, the writer can begin to decide what will be his or her best stance or viewpoint to adopt.

The writer may choose to remain the detached observer, one who

8.6

merely records what is seen but who relies on his selection of the facts and the ordering of them to achieve the desired response from the audience. At least the writer can then pose as an honest broker who criticises without prejudice and 'without sneering, teaches the rest to sneer'. Many a play has had its run cut short because of bad critical notices after the first night. Often, however, the character of the critic and the context in which he or she is writing become more obvious than the topic at the centre of the critical piece. Consider the conclusion of George Orwell's criticism of Winston Churchill's book on the Second World War, *Their Finest Hour*. It was probably the last review Orwell (the author of *Animal Farm*) wrote; this conclusion shows more of Orwell than it does of Churchill and his book:

> Whether or not 1940 was anyone else's finest hour, it was certainly not Churchill's. However much one may disagree with him, however thankful one may be that he and his party did not win the 1945 election, one has to admire in him not only his courage but also a certain largeness and geniality which came out even in formal memoirs of this type. The British people have generally rejected his policies, but they have always had a liking for him, as one can see from the tone of the stories about him that have been told throughout most of his life. Often, no doubt, these stories were apocryphal and sometimes they were also unprintable, but the fact of their circulating is significant. At the time of the Dunkirk evacuation, for instance, when Churchill made his often-quoted fighting speech, it was rumoured that what he actually said, when recording the speech for broadcasting, was: 'We will fight on the beaches, we will fight in the streets . . . We'll throw bottles at the b-s, it's about all we've got left' – but, of course, the B.B.C.'s switch-censor pressed his thumb on the key at the right moment. One may assume that this story is untrue, but at the time it was felt that it ought to be true. It was a fitting tribute from ordinary people to the tough and humorous old man whom they would not accept as a peace-time leader but whom in the moment of disaster they felt to be representative of themselves.

One of the most effective ways of being critical in writing is to use satire. The satirist is, as Kenneth Tynan said of Bernard Shaw, 'a demolition expert'. Part of his art is to appear to be writing from one position when in fact he is writing from quite another. Daniel Defoe and Henry Fielding, George Orwell and Evelyn Waugh are names of novelists that quickly spring to mind as satirists who use this method from the world of English Literature. Defoe makes Robinson Crusoe, for example, a Christian gentleman who seeks to re-establish on his desert island the very conditions of eighteenth-century Christian England from which good fortune had delivered him by means of the shipwreck; he even makes Man Friday wear linen drawers, a jerkin and a cap. Implicitly and satirically, Defoe is commenting on those writers (e.g. Aphra Behn in her novel *Oroonoko* (c. 1678) who were beginning to argue that some races were suppressed by Western civilisation and that man in his natural state was purer and nearer to God than man in so-called civilised society. Much of Defoe's writing was ironical and satirical; much of his art rested on assuming in his writing a position he was attempting to abolish. In 1702 he produced a pamphlet, *The Shortest Way with Dissenters*, which seriously seemed to demand the total suppression of all those who did not accept the Established Church – even their execution and yet Defoe was himself a dissenter or nonconformist!

Successful satirical writing needs a careful evaluation of the point of view used by the writer, the careful selection of facts to be used, a sound judgement about the context in which the writing is to appear, and a good understanding of the audience at which it is aimed. To master this art is to achieve success in what may well be the most difficult kind of directed writing.

Personal writing

For a full discussion of this aspect of writing see **Chapter 2** (pp. 16–31). | 8.7

Dramatic writing

For a full discussion of this aspect of writing see **Chapter 3** (pp. 34–46). | 8.8

Exercises

1 Write a *narrative* composition of about 450 words on *one* of the following topics. (Decide on your point of view, the 'slanting' of your writing towards your reader(s), and the arrangement of the events in the story *before you begin*. Take care with spelling, punctuation, and grammar.)

    a) A funny thing happened to me today on the way to school . . .
    b) The hole in the road.
    c) Going round the bend.

d) The day time stood still.
e) The hunter became the hunted.

2 Write a discursive (discussion) composition of about 450 words on *one* of the following topics. (Select and order your material careful-ly; decide on your point of view and maintain it; direct your arguments at your reader with the deliberate intention of persuading him or her to accept your views or of provoking a strong reaction. Take care with spelling, punctuation, and grammar.)

a) Co-education is bad for both boys and girls.
b) The school-leaving age should be lowered to 13.
c) 'Do not waste your time on social questions; what is the matter with the poor is Poverty: what is the matter with the rich is Uselessness.' (G. B. Shaw)
d) 'Do not do unto others as you would they should do unto you. Their tastes may not be the same.' (G. B. Shaw)
e)   'To-thine own self be-true,
And it must follow as the night the day
Thou canst not then be false to any man.'
(Shakespeare: *Hamlet*)

3   a) Using the table given in 8.3a above, p. 112, write a statement in about 50 words about the emphasis on different parts of the pupils' work that is shown by the homework they were set.
b) Design and draw up a displayed advertisement to be inserted in a newspaper for a well-known food product which you use regularly.
c) Study the map set out in 8.3c above, p. 114, and then, *in not more than 200 words*, use the information it gives for an account to be included in a history textbook of the movements of the Norman army immediately following the Battle of Hastings.
d) Study the graph given in 8.3d above, p. 115. Then make a statement *in about 150 words* about differences between the ways in which 12-year-olds and 14-year-olds are grouped in schools.
e) With the help of a diagram or map draw up and entry in an attractive brochure intended to show visitors how to find the main assembly hall once they have arrived at your school or college.
f) Write up, for inclusion as an article in a cookery book for housewives, the recipe for a dish which you particularly like cooking (or eating).

4 Read carefully 8.4 above, pp. 117–8, and then write a description of *either* a person *or* a place *or* a process as a possible paragraph for inclusion in a novel. (You might like to choose a topic which other members of your class or group should be able to recognise immediately. Read out your work when it is finished to see if they do show any signs of recognition.)

5 Imagine that you are the Sales Director of a firm about to launch a nationwide campaign to sell a range of plastic toys to keep bored household pets amused (e.g. moulded cats for dogs to chew; moving mice for cats to chase; hawks in natural colours to keep caged canaries alert and singing). Write a letter which will be dropped through every letter box in the country as part of your sales campaign intended *to persuade* potential customers to buy your worthless but expensive products.

6 Write a passionate speech which is intended to persuade your audience of non-involved and docile people to adopt a political *or* a religious belief which you feel strongly about. (See 8.5, pp. 118–9, to give you some examples of persuasive writing.)

7 Re-write the speech you produced in Exercise **6** in a more subtle way for the same audience, making use of irony, satire, and understatement in order to persuade them to take up your views.

8 Read 8.6, pp. 119–21, carefully and then write a critical review for inclusion in the columns of a quality Sunday newspaper of a film, a play, or a TV programme you have seen *or* of a book or magazine you have read recently.
(For exercises on personal or dramatic writing see pp. 16–31 and pp. 36–46 above respectively.)

9 Directed Reading

> 'Do not read as children do to amuse yourself, or like the ambitious, for the purpose of instruction. No, read in order to live.'
>
> Gustave Flaubert

Just as we never write without a purpose, so **we never read without a purpose**. Most people read much more often than they write; it is as well, therefore, to be clear about the objectives we have in directing our reading at one text rather than at another. The purpose of our reading will determine how we read.

Flaubert, in the quotation at the head of this chapter, isolated the three main purposes we have in reading:

a) pleasure;
b) information;
c) interpretation.

Let us consider these purposes in turn.

Reading for pleasure

9.1

The cynic might say 'Reading is sometimes an ingenious device for avoiding thought' (Sir Arthur Helps, 1813–75). Others have acknowledged that it provides a profound source of pleasure for many.

The speed of reading a book or a passage is important. Sometimes it is best to read fast or to 'skim' the text; at other times it is necessary to read slowly (and to re-read) in order to understand meaning. In reading for pleasure the speed will need to vary according to the writer's **point of view**, the **topic** and the **context**; it is important not merely to read the words but also to go beneath their surface, to make connections, and to see significance. For example, in reading fiction for pleasure the reader needs to move at a pace which will allow him or her to:

a) recognise the angle from which the writer is writing; this may change significantly within a matter of paragraphs;

b) to follow the sequence in which the events happen;

c) to connect the facts, happenings, comments, and characters which make up the whole complex tapestry of the story;

d) to make inferences from descriptions, settings, actions, observations given in the text;

e) to recognise the level on which the story is being told and spot humour, climax, satire, irony, etc.;

f) to interpret figurative language and symbols as part of the effect of the narrative;

g) to see the composition of the story and to draw inferences from what is said or done, within the framework of the story.

In reading poetry or imaginative prose the reader needs to be particularly aware of the level on which the writer is operating. Take, for example, the opening sentence of James Joyce's short story, *The Dead*: **9.2**

Lily, the caretaker's daughter, was literally run off her feet.

The significance of the girl's name in relation to the subject of the story makes an immediate impact. The word *literally* is used colloquially to mean 'absolutely, quite, completely' and yet it clashes with the figurative phrase 'run off her feet'; one simply cannot be *literally* 'run off one's feet'. It is clear, then, that the tension between the ordinary, everyday fact and the symbolism of the language will be a major feature of the story. The careful reader moves, therefore, slowly enough through the story to see such significant details and to respond to them. The appreciation of the story on a multiplicity of levels is the greater because of the sensitivity demanded of the reader.

Part of the pleasure of some reading lies in escape. Science fiction creates a world remote from our own into which the reader can fly. At the same time, however, the careful writer makes implicit and strong links between his or her world of fantasy and the reader's own 'real' world; it is for the reader to make his own connections between them. This kind of writing allows a writer to isolate specific features of human behaviour that should be examined. In *The Large Ant*, for example, written by Howard Fast in 1960, a fisherman struck an insect dead as he lay in bed alone in a hunting shack. The insect, it later appears, was a fourteen or fifteen-inch long ant. What seemed to be the thorax of the ant was dissected: **9.3**

it came open like the belly of a bomber; it was a pocket, a pouch, a receptacle that the thing wore, and in it were four beautiful little tools or instruments or weapons, each about an inch and a half long. They were beautiful the way any object of functional purpose and loving creation is beautiful – the way the creature itself would have been beautiful, had it not been an insect and myself a man . . . I had to look at the ant now, and I realised that I had not truly looked at it before. *We don't look carefully at a thing that is horrible or repugnant to us. You can't look at anything through a screen of hatred.*

The ant emerges as a phenomenally beautiful and intricate creature as the dissection continues. The killer begins to question the human instinct to kill what it fears or does not recognise. The point made by the sentences italicised above is driven home in the story as it unfolds. The levels of meaning on which any good, imaginative writing operates readily establish themselves.

Reading for information

9.4

This is the most common purpose we have in using our reading skills: to find facts. Telephone directories, encyclopaedias, text books, dictionaries, recipe books, workshop manuals, guidebooks, phrase books in foreign languages, railway or bus timetables, instructions on the wrappers of cans of food, and bank statements – all provide us with the details we need for life in the twentieth century.

Sometimes the facts are easy to arrive at and at other times need to be scrutinised closely; some material is supported by other visual signs, diagrams, and illustrations, and some dispenses with words altogether (e.g. some road signs set out in *The Highway Code*).

9.5

Newspapers and magazines present facts, but the moment one word or phrase is selected rather than another, one detail is omitted rather than another, the factual nature of the writing becomes nearer comment. It is for the reader to pick up the signs of such interpretations in presenting facts.

Words, too, carry connotations which go beyond their straightforward dictionary meanings. The fact that English is so rich in words with similar meanings (*synonyms*) provides a rich storehouse of interpretations. Consider, for example, some of the words available to indicate *dislike*: hate, abhorrence, coolness, enmity, hostility, animosity, resentment, grudge, spite, venom, bitterness, malice; disgust, aversion, repugnance, repulsion, antipathy, disapproval. (See also **Chapter 7**, Exercise **2**, p. 104.) Similarly, the *phrasing* of expressions of dislike can operate on a number of different levels:

How I loathe the dress!
I've seen much better.
Really, I'd have preferred something different.

I never want to see it again.
I simply dislike it.
It fills me with revulsion.
Is there an alternative?
No thanks!

Signs

These may be with or without words but they are usually intended to provide instant recognition and immediate response from the reader. Consider the following signs. Can you say what each means?

9.6

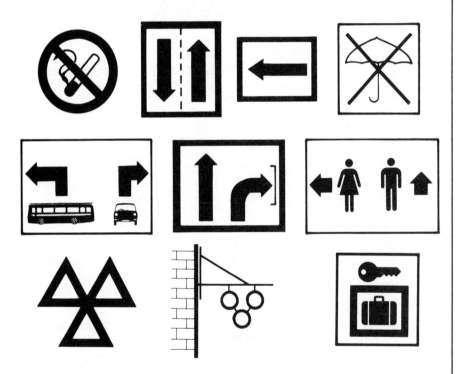

Instruction manuals

These usually combine diagrams and comments. The words are closely linked to the diagram; they are kept to a minimum but they do require close reference to the illustration if they are to be understood.
   e.g.

9.7

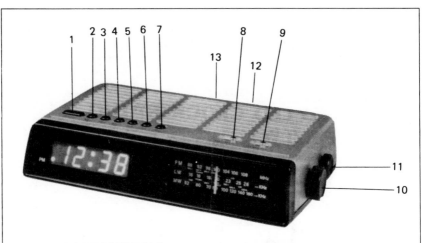

LOCATION OF CONTROLS

1. Snooze Bar
2. Alarm Off Button
3. Sleep Button
4. Alarm Set Button
5. Time Set Button
6. Fast Forward Button
7. Slow Forward Button
8. Radio Automatic/Off/On Switch
9. LM/MW/FM Waveband Switch
10. Tuning Control
11. Volume Control
12. Buzzer On/Off Switch
13. Clock Brightness Switch

DO NOT REMOVE COVER WITHOUT FIRST DISCONNECTING UNIT FROM THE MAINS SUPPLY. THIS EQUIPMENT SHOULD BE DISCON-NECTED FROM THE MAINS WHEN NOT IN USE.
IT IS RECOMMENDED THAT THIS UNIT IS NOT USED IN VERY HOT OR HUMID CONDITIONS.

ELECTRONIC CLOCK OPERATION

1. This clock radio operates on 240V AC 50Hz. Connect the bare ends of the lead to a plug fused with a 3 amp fuse and plug into an appropriate socket.
2. The set is now working as an electronic clock and it will flash the clock figures to show you it is not set correctly.
3. To set the correct time, press buttons 5 and 6 together. When the time is nearly correct press buttons 5 and 7 together. When the correct hour and minute is showing, stop pressing.
4. Your clock is a red digital 12 hour and the indication that it is PM is shown by a red dot appearing in the bottom left hand corner. If no red dot appears, then the time is set to AM.

Timetables

9.8

These include TV guides, telephone directories, recipe books, etc. The layout of the entries here is of considerable importance. The context within which the reader is consulting the document will usually make the details clear, but the aim of the writer will be to present facts clearly, adequately, and attractively so that the reader will understand, select and interpret, and respond quickly and without anxiety. Diagrams are not usually necessary.

e.g.

LONDON-PARIS – NIGHTLINER SERVICE **121**

DLY	T = Toilet Halt				Fares From LONDON & DOVER			
					Adults Students Children			
					Fares To 31.5.83		Fares From 1.6.83	
					S	R	S	R
2100	Dep.	**LONDON**, Victoria Coach Station Bay 18	Arr.	0730				
2315	Arr.	DOVER, P & O Ferries	Dep.	0515				
2359	Dep.	Booking Hall, Eastern Docks	Arr.	0445				
0515	Arr.	(T) AMIENS, SNCF Railway Stn. (T)	Dep.	0045				
0715	Arr.	**PARIS**, VIA Coach Station, Place Stalingrad	Dep.	2230	14.50	26.00	16.00	28.50

LONDON-PARIS – DAYLINER SERVICE **122**

APR1 JUN 21	JUN25 SEP 30		APR1 –JUN 23	JUN25 -SEP 30	Fares From LONDON & DOVER			
					Adults Students Children			
WED SAT	DLY	See also service 151 for additional Day Services between London & Paris			Fares To 31.5.83		Fares From 1.6.83	
					S	R	S	R
0830	0830	Dep. **LONDON**, Victoria Coach Station Bay 18	1630 Arr.	1630				
1100	1100	Arr. DOVER, P & O Ferries	1430 Dep.	1430				
1200	1200	Dep. Booking Hall, Eastern Docks	1400 Arr.	1400				
1900	1900	Arr. **PARIS**, VIA Coach Station, Place Stalingrad	0930 Dep.	0930	14.50	26.00	16.00	28.50
			THUR SAT	DLY				

LONDON-LISBON SERVICE **121/1**

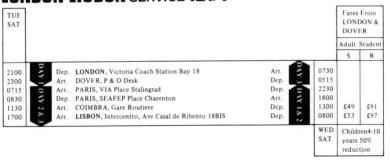

TUE SAT				Fares From LONDON & DOVER	
				Adult Student	
				S	R
2100	Dep. **LONDON**, Victoria Coach Station Bay 18	Arr.	0730		
2300	Arr. DOVER, P & O Desk	Dep.	0515		
0715	Arr. PARIS, VIA Place Stalingrad	Dep.	2230		
0830	Dep. PARIS, SEAFEP Place Charenton	Arr.	1800		
1130	Arr. COIMBRA, Gare Routiere	Dep.	1300	£49	£91
1700	Arr. **LISBON**, Intercentro, Ave Casal de Ribeiro 18BIS	Dep.	0800	£53	£97
			WED SAT	Children 4-10 years 50% reduction	

Reading and interpretation

Here, the art of reading concentrates on the selection of material and the efficient, clear summarising of facts. Again, the context (e.g.

9.9

preparation for an examination, homework) and the purpose for which the notes are intended will condition how detailed the reading needs to be. Often the general reader will go to a reference book with a specific question he or she wants answered, e.g. someone with a wart on the hand might consult a medical book in order to find out what might have caused it and how it could be removed. The student, however, is faced with the problems of what and how much to summarise from the books available on a subject. At the time of an examination he or she needs clear, concentrated material which will recall what has been absorbed more profoundly, although lost for the moment from immediate recall.

It is useful to acquire two speeds of reading (see also **Chapter 10**, pp. 147–55): fast (skimming) and slow. The efficient student will have trained himself or herself to leaf through books quite quickly in order to spot items that are of concern; the list of contents, chapter headings, and the index will prove invaluable here. Once a text has been chosen as of importance, the notes from it should first set out the full title, the author, the date of publication and the edition of the book. Any comments taken from it word for word should be enclosed in inverted commas, so that if you use them later you can acknowledge them properly; it is very easy for your notes to become part of a final essay and unless you acknowledge all your direct quotations you may be accused of plagiarism. Define the topic of the chapter and note the point of view of the writer. It is often useful to set out notes with major and minor sub-headings on a page, with the facts numbered.

If you make your notes look orderly on the page it will be far easier to remember them when you need them, since many students have excellent visual memories. Constantly select and condense; organise your material; do not attempt to summarise everything in the book. The secret of good note-making for examinations and studying is to try to put yourself into your own place several months ahead. What will be needed then? How useful will what is being done now seem then?

Reading and précis

9.10

A précis of a passage usually consists of the reduction of a passage, a chapter, or even a book; it is concerned with keeping the salient facts clear. It is important that the sense of the text and the viewpoint of the writer are established by a *first*, careful reading. Conclusions about these matters should be tested by a *second* detailed reading. When the notes for the final draft of the précis are being made it is best not to reproduce exactly phrases from the original writing and to avoid illustrations, examples and repetitions. The tone and direction of the original writing are best kept in the final draft wherever possible.

Take, for example, the following passage on additives to food available to the public. It is written from an objective standpoint and contains details which merely serve as examples to the main points. A possible précis follows which keeps the tone of the passage, brings out the facts (keeping, incidentally, the order of the original), and reduces the extract to about a third of its length.

In August, 1860, an Act was passed making it an offence knowingly to sell food containing an ingredient injurious to health, or food which was adulterated. This was the first general law of its kind in the world.

The Act of 1860 gave powers to local authorities to appoint an analyst – but this was not compulsory – and any purchaser of food and drink was entitled to have it analysed (provided an analyst was available) for a sum 'not less than 2s. 6d. – and not more than 10s. 6d.'. Food adulteration had been commonly practised long before the nineteenth century, and ineffectual attempts had been made earlier through the passing of statutes to safeguard the quality of pepper, tea, coffee, chocolate, beer, and wine, and to stop the practice of adding lead chromate to confectionery. In 1758 the addition of alum to bread was forbidden. The Act of 1860 was more successful than the statutes which preceded it, but it was still not strong enough, because it called for voluntary co-operative action, which was not readily forthcoming.

The modern successor of this nineteenth-century legislation – the Food and Drugs Act of 1955, with a number of additional regulations – aims at the prevention of health hazards to the consumer, and also at the prevention of fraud. Sampling officers, appointed by local authorities, keep an eye on foodstuffs on sale in shops and on market stalls. They purchase samples, which are then examined by the public analyst, who also deals with complaints made directly by the public. Such complaints mainly concern nails, flies or beetles found in food, or that 'mysterious substance left in the bottom of the teacup'. It is less common for the public to complain of quality, ingredients or handling.

Nearly all present-day food manufacturers are aware of their responsibilities and have achieved high standards of food purity. Highly developed apparatus and instruments provide the means for the control of purity, quality, preparation, processing, and packaging, as well as for storage and distribution of their products. As a result, a wide choice of pure foods is offered to the public, and the proportion of samples submitted to one public analyst in 1959 found to be 'adulterated or otherwise giving rise to irregularity' under the Food and Drugs Act was only 4 per cent (113 out of 2,763 samples analysed).

But should there have been this 4 per cent – and how many others remained undetected? It lies largely in the hands of the consumer to ensure that pure food is not only covered by legislation, but that it becomes an accepted and effective standard. There are still relatively few people who are prepared to take action about food of poor quality served under unhygienic conditions. As long as people are reluctant to complain, carelessness may often go unnoticed and unrebuked, and there may remain opportunities for the unscrupulous.

e.g. Précis

In 1860, the first general law against the sale of harmful or adulterated food enabled local authorities to appoint analysts, so that purchasers of food could have it analysed for which they would pay. This Act was more successful than earlier statutes against specific abuses, but its weakness was its dependence on voluntary action.

The Food and Drugs Act of 1955, intended to safeguard health and prevent fraud, provides for officers to make sample purchase and submit them to the public analyst, who deals also with the public's complaints, though these usually concern the presence of foreign bodies rather than bad quality or handling.

Today most food manufacturers carefully control the purity and quality of their products, and one analyst in 1959 found only four per cent of his samples defective. But standards could be improved if consumers were readier to report defective food or service. Otherwise the careless and unscrupulous remain undetected.

Reading and summary

9.11

(See also R. A. Banks and F. D. A. Burns, *Summary and Directed Writing*, Hodder and Stoughton, 1980, for a full discussion of how to tackle Summaries and how to direct them at a specific audience.)

The skill to read a passage carefully, or to study an argument, or to examine a document closely, and then to extract from it details for a specific purpose is one often needed in our daily lives. This skill depends on the ability to read very closely what is on the page, to understand its meaning and significance within its own context, to determine the viewpoint of the writer, and to recognise what is relevant and what is not. The ability to re-arrange these facts and to re-direct them at a specific audience is one acquired only by experience.

The purpose of a summary may be to present ideas factually, to persuade others, to produce a balanced argument, to amuse or interest the reader, to explain or to instruct. The purpose needs to be clearly established before the summary is made, since it will determine the shape and form of the final draft. The basic skill, however, lies in the ability to select and arrange material accurately and relevantly. Sometimes the material to be summarised uses statistical tables, graphs, maps, diary entries, etc.

Take, for example, the following passage set in a recent national examination. Candidates were asked to write an article for inclusion in a local newspaper 'deliberately setting out to persuade readers that noise is a real threat to everyone in today's society'. It should consist of *three* paragraphs as follows:

a) deploring the potential dangers of noise in modern life;
b) suggesting how the dangers can be reduced or eliminated;
c) admitting that it is neither possible nor desirable to eliminate all noise in life.

Only the information given in the passage and table was to be used but the style had to be that appropriate to a local newspaper and the declared intention of the article was to *persuade*.

Noise

The unit in which noise is measured is known as the *decibel* (db). The threshold of hearing, that is the point at which man has the capacity to hear, is at zero decibels; somewhere around 180 decibels is the lethal level. Rats exposed to levels approaching this turn cannibalistic and eventually die from heart failure; short exposure to 150 db can permanently damage the human ear and cause excruciating pain; slightly lower levels can cause temporary deafness and if there is a long-term exposure to noise above that found near a motorway where traffic is continually passing there is a grave risk of permanent hearing-loss and nervous exhaustion.

Table: Common noise levels

Jet aircraft at 200 feet near a large airport	150 db
Pneumatic drill	130 db
A 'hard-rock' band	115 db
Power mower; accelerating motor-cycle	110 db
Food mixer (2 to 4 feet away)	100 db
Underground train (inside)	100 db
Heavy city traffic	90 db

Passenger cars on nearby motorway	65–86 db
Normal conversation	60–70 db
Telephone conversation	60 db
Quiet residential street noises	50 db
Tick of watch (2 feet away)	30 db
Leaves rustling in the wind	10 db

It is best, of course, to minimise the potential danger from noise at its source; much of it is within our control in the kitchen, living-room, and the play or work-room. Dishwashers, food-mixers, tumble-driers, electric drills, and washing-machines can raise the noise level to dangerous levels but if they are placed and operated in rooms separate from the living accommodation the noise level is reduced or even eliminated; if the machines are stood on sound-absorbing pads the nuisance and risk are diminished. The acoustic power of a full orchestra is rarely more than ten watts and yet music systems used in some living rooms can produce sounds at more than a hundred watts of audio power. Young people, too, often feel it necessary to amplify the sound of their musical instruments and they also plug their transistor outputs into their ears with the volume turned up at full blast. Perhaps they want to follow Beethoven into deafness.

Most television sets are turned up to dangerous levels whilst the viewers' attention is distracted from the threat by the picture flashing in front of their eyes. Noisy dustbins, squeaky gates or machines strangers to the oil-can, loud lawn-mowers shattering the peace of suburban afternoons, honking car-horns, and children reliving the latest TV Western in the street, all contribute to the noise pollution of our own time. Curtains, carpets, large furniture, and wall-fittings help to reduce noise levels within the home by their deadening effect; outdoors, trees and shrubs, high walls and fences act as noise-breaks; even lawns and flower-borders make the environment quieter just as carpets reduce sound levels indoors.

However, there are those who think that noise is preferable to washing clothes by hand, cutting grass with scythes, and walking long distances. Noise, they argue, is a necessary part of man's advance. One man's noise is another's sweet melody. Some think that a crying baby, the explosive roar from a motor-bike's exhaust, the throbbing beat of a pop-group, or the rattling of bells as cows slither down idyllic mountain slopes are all beautiful sounds. The living world is full of sounds; only the world of the dead is uniformly silent.

The following suggests a summary of the selected relevant facts that might be used in the article. Try to rewrite them slanting the article directly at the audience of a local newspaper.

DEAD OR DEAF?

a) *Deploring the potential dangers of noise in modern life:*
At about 180 decibels a noise can kill and even a short exposure to 150 db (about the noise of a jet aircraft) can damage
hearing and cause terrible pain. Levels between 100 and 120 db
can produce temporary deafness but long-term exposure to
noises as low as 80 db can lead to permanent hearing loss
and nervous exhaustion. There is a serious risk in the home
from machines such as dishwashers, food-mixers, tumble driers
and electric drills as well as powerful audio systems and TV's
turned up too loudly.

b) *Suggesting how the dangers can be reduced or eliminated:*
It is best to eliminate noise at its source; most noises are under
our control. Domestic machines should be separated from
living accommodation and might be stood on sound-
absorbing pads. The volume on transistors and TVs should be
turned down; indoors curtains, carpets, large furniture and
wall-fittings and outdoors trees, shrubs, walls, fences and
flower beds help to reduce noise.

c) *Admitting it is neither possible nor desirable to eliminate all
noise in life:*
Most noises are below serious danger level and can be
reduced or eliminated. This is preferable to denying progress.
Noise is part of life today; some noises are thought beautiful –
a crying baby, the roar of motor bikes, or pop groups. Only the
dead are silent.

Reading and interpretation

9.12

Much of what we read invites some comment and interpretation – or at
least our response. It is useful, therefore, to be sensitive to the
'indicators' or 'signs' that condition our reactions.

Advertisers often bring together two unrelated ideas in order to allow
the reader to make his or her own associations. In the early days of
television cigarette advertising, a single young man in a bleak deserted
street lit a cigarette in the midst of a warm glow from a lighted match
beneath the caption: *You are never alone with a Strand.* The suggestion
that some personal problems might be resolved by smoking was
implicit without being justified. More recently counter-advertising has
inverted the appeal of some marketing material: one car company has
advertised the merits of a competitors' vehicle in order to show the
advantages of its own product.

Our own thoughts and feelings, ideas and experiences are brought
to bear on what we read. We associate the words on the page with
ourselves in interpreting the evaluating them. This is particularly true
in the reading of poetry or imaginative prose, where words within a
context operate on a number of different levels. Notice in the following
how the meaning of the word 'rest' shifts a number of times in the
following poem written in the seventeenth century:

THE PULLEY

When God at first made man,
Having a glass of blessings standing by,
'Let us,' said he, 'pour on him all we can;
Let the world's riches, which dispersed lie,
    Contract into a span.'

So strength first made a way;
Then beauty flowed, then wisdom, humour, pleasure;
When almost all was out, God made a stay,
Perceiving that alone of all his treasures
    Rest in the bottom lay.

'For if I should,' said he,
'Bestow this jewel also on my creature,
He would adore my gifts instead of me,
And rest in Nature, not the God of Nature.
    So both should losers be.

Yet let him keep the rest,
But keep them with repining restlessness;
Let him be rich and weary, that at least,
If goodness lead him not, yet weariness
    May toss him to my breast.'

George Herbert

Can you see why the poem is called *The Pulley*? What is the basic
comparison that the poet is using in describing the way God created
man endowed with his blessings? How closely can you associate what
the poet is saying about the spiritual restlessness of men and women
with your own experience?

The problem sometimes arises when the reader thinks that what is
printed must be true. 'I read it in the paper' or 'I read it in a book' are
arguments sometimes put forward to justify views. It is worth re-
membering that newspapers can be slanted (compare advertisements)
to make their readers accept one view rather than another, and that
books can be wrong. *Reading is an active occupation.* Interpretation
and response demand alertness from the reader. Once again, the
'audience' is just as much part of the reading activity, along with the

writer's point of view, the topic, and the context, as it is of the writing activity.

Test your alertness in reading by finding the fallacies in the following arguments from *Alice's Adventures in Wonderland*:

'You should say what you mean,' the March Hare went on.

'I do,' Alice hastily replied; 'at least – at least I mean what I say – that's the same thing, you know.'

'Not the same thing a bit!' said the Hatter. 'Why, you might just as well say that "I see what I eat" is the same thing as "I eat what I see"!'

'You might just as well say,' added the March Hare, 'that "I like what I get" is the same thing as "I get what I like"!'

'You might just as well say,' added the Dormouse which seemed to be talking in its sleep, 'that "I breathe when I sleep" is the same thing as "I sleep when I breathe"!'

'It *is* the same thing with you,' said the Hatter, and here the conversation dropped, and the party sat silent for a minute.

Exercises

1 Read the following passage **quickly** and say how many times the point of view of the writer changes. Then read the passage **slowly** to establish more precisely *where* it changes and *how* these changes affect the impact of the writing on you as the reader:

A dreadful peal of thunder shook the house, a strain of unearthly music floated through the air, a panel at the top of the staircase flew back with a loud noise, and out on the landing, looking very pale and white, stepped Virginia.

'Good heavens, child, where have you been?' said Mr Otis, thinking that she had been playing some foolish trick on them. 'You must never play these practical jokes any more.'

'Except on the Ghost! Except on the Ghost!' shrieked the twins as they capered about.

'My own darling, thank God you are found; you must never leave my side again,' murmured Mrs Otis, as she kissed the trembling child.

'Papa,' said Virginia quietly, 'I have been with the Ghost.'

The whole family gazed at her in mute amazement.

2 Read 9.2 and 9.3. Then write *either* a ghost story *or* a science fiction story which changes on a number of occasions the point of

view from which the narrative is given. (Try to confine yourself to not more than 450 words.)

3   a) Consult your local telephone directory and look up your own surname. Then find someone with the same surname that lives closest to you. What are the initials, the address, and the telephone number of the person?

b) Look up the meanings of the following words in a good dictionary. Copy out the definitions as carefully and as accurately as you can:

a) *bellarmine;*	b) *chrestomathy;*
c) *desquamate;*	d) *gaberlunzie;*
e) *halbstarker;*	f) *kinetheodolite;*
g) *laeotropic;*	h) *mattoid;*
i) *nyctophobia;*	j) *wonga-wonga.*

4 Invent some signs (which use no words) to indicate the following:

a) Swimming is dangerous.
b) Do not lean out of the window.
c) Keep out! Unexploded bomb!
d) No smoking. Maximum penalty Death!
e) Climbing of trees not allowed.
f) No cycling on the pavement.
g) Police check-point ahead.
h) Fancy dress obligatory.
i) Ghosts crossing. Watch out!
J) No noise please; you are entering a silent zone.

5   a) Draw a watch which:

i) gives the time digitally;
ii) gives the day and the month;
iii) acts as a stop-watch;
iv) can be wound manually.

b) Label the four controls relating to a) i–iv above.
c) Explain, by reference to your diagram, how to adjust the time, alter the day and the month, use the stop-watch facilities, and wind up the watch.

6 Using the information set out in the timetable below, answer the following questions:

a) How long would the journey take from London to Marbella on Friday, 3 June?
b) How much would a return ticket from London to Cordoba cost a student?
c) Can you suggest the probable reason why the return coach

from Lourdes to London between 16 June and 3 October leaves only on a Friday?

d) How much approximately would the total return fare be for a mother and father, their son aged eleven and twin daughters aged seven for a return trip from London to Torremolinos?

SERVICE 181

LONDON-MADRID-ALGECIRAS via Bordeaux

Operated by Wallace Arnold/SCETA/VIA/SEAFEP/Linebus

Fares From LONDON & DOVER

Station		ADULT S	ADULT R	STUDENT S	STUDENT R
LONDON, Victoria Coach Station, Bay 18	Dep.				£46
DOVER, P&O Desk Booking Hall, Eastern Docks	Arr.				
PARIS, VIA Coach Station, Place Stalingrad	Dep.				
PARIS, SEAFIP Coach Station, Charenton	Dep.				
TOURS, SNCF Railway Station	Arr.	£28	£51	£24	
BORDEAUX, Francebus, 32 Rue Charles Domecq	Dep.				£57
BIARRITZ, SNCF Railway Station	Arr.	£34	£63	£31	£67
ST JEAN DE LUZ, SNCF Railway Station	Arr.	£40	£75	£36	£67
BAYONNE (Transfer coaches)	Arr.	£40	£75	£36	
PAU, SNCF Railway Station	Arr.	£40	£75	£36	£67
TARBES, SCETA Coach Station	Arr.	£40	£75	£36	£67
LOURDES, Turpin Agency, 19 Ave. Paradis	Arr.	£40	£75	£36	£67
SAN SEBASTIAN, Renfe Railway Station	Arr.	£43	£80	£39	£73
VITORIA, Linebus Estacion Autobuses c/Francia	Arr.	£43	£80	£39	£73
BURGOS, Linebus Estacion Autobuses c/Miranda	Arr.	£43	£80	£39	£73
MADRID, Linebus Estacion Sur Autobuses	Arr.	£43	£80	£39	£73
CalleCanarias 17/Underground-Palos de Moguer	Dep.	£52	£97	£47	£88
CORDOBA, Hotel Melia, Jardines De La Victoria	Arr.	£64	£120	£57	£107
MALAGA, In front of Renfe Railway Station	Dep.	£70	£131	£64	£119
TORREMOLINOS, Iberbus Road Malaga Cadiz (Junction with Calle Hoyo)	Dep.	£70	£131	£64	£119
FUENGIROLA, In front of Autocars Portillo, Road Malaga Cadiz	Arr.	£70	£131	£64	£119
MARBELLA, In front of Cafeteria Sport, Junction Avda Ramon/Cajal	Arr.	£70	£131	£64	£119
ALGECIRAS, Linebus, Bus Esplanade Estacion Maritime Taquilla 45	Arr.	£73	£135	£66	£122

Children 4 – 10 years approx. 40% reduction of adult fares

An exercise in précis-writing (1)

7 The following passage contains about 500 words. Summarise it in 160–170 words, *avoiding as far as possible the original language of the passage*. Give at the end the exact number of words in the summary.

Almost from the moment of its creation a volcanic island is foredoomed to destruction. It has in itself the seeds of its own dissolution, for new explosions, or landslides of the soft soil, may violently accelerate its disintegration. Whether the destruction of an island comes quickly or only after long ages of geologic time may also depend on external forces; the rains that wear away the loftiest of land mountains, the sea, and even man himself.

Sometimes the disintegration takes abrupt and violent form. The greatest explosion of historic time was the destruction of the island of Krakatoa. In 1680 there had been a premonitory eruption on this small island in Sunda Strait, between Java and Sumatra in the Netherlands Indies. Two hundred years later there had been a series of earthquakes. In the spring of 1883, smoke and steam began to ascend from fissures in the volcanic cone. The ground became noticeably warm, and warning rumblings and hissings came from the volcano. Then, on 27 August, Krakatoa literally exploded. In an appalling series of eruptions, that lasted two days, the whole northern half of the cone was carried away. The sudden inrush of ocean water added the fury of superheated steam to the cauldron. When the inferno of white-hot lava, molten rock, steam, and smoke had finally subsided, the island that had stood 1,400 feet above the sea had become a cavity a thousand feet below sea level. Only along one edge of the former crater did a remnant of the island remain.

Krakatoa, in its destruction, became known to the entire world. The eruption caused a hundred-foot wave that wiped out villages along the Strait and killed people by tens of thousands. The wave was felt on the shores of the Indian Ocean and at Cape Horn; rounding the Cape into the Atlantic, it sped northward and retained its identity even as far as the English Channel. The sound of the explosions was heard in the Philippine Islands, in Australia, and on the island of Madagascar, nearly 3,000 miles away. And the clouds of volcanic dust, the pulverised rock that had been torn from the heart of Krakatoa, ascended into the stratosphere and were carried around the globe to give rise to a series of spectacular sunsets in every country of the world for near a year.

Although Krakatoa's dramatic passing was the most violent eruption that modern man has witnessed, Krakatoa itself seems to have been the product of an even greater one. There is evidence that an immense volcano once stood where the waters of Sunda Strait now lie. In some remote period a titanic explosion blew it away, leaving only its base represented by a broken chain of islands. The largest of these was Krakatoa, which, in its own demise, carried away what was left of the original crater ring. But in 1929 a new volcanic island arose in this place – Anak Krakatoa, Child of Krakatoa.

An exercise in précis-writing (2)

8 Summarise, *in your own words as far as possible*, the following passage (which contains about 430 words), reducing it to between 140 and 150 words. State at the end the *exact* number of words your have used.

The Mosquito in Africa

Of all the world's trouble-makers, it is doubtful if any could exceed the record of the mosquito, the carrier of the germs which cause malaria, yellow fever, and several other deadly diseases. Not only do many people die of malaria, but countless others are so weakened by it that they cannot cultivate their fields properly. Lacking enough food and without energy, they easily fall victim to other diseases.

Africa is not, of course, the only continent to be plagued by malaria-carrying mosquitoes. They abound in most tropical lands, especially where there is stagnant water. They are found, too, in some cooler countries, and there was some malaria even in Britain during the last century, until the marshlands were gradually drained.

The word 'malaria' simply means 'bad air', for the illness was thought to be due in some way to the heavy, dank air particularly common in marshes at night. But the real link is the mosquito, whose favourite breeding-haunts lie in such places. Not every mosquito, however, carries the malaria germ, and indeed the insect only passes on the germs if it has first bitten and sucked the blood of a person already infected with the disease.

The complete life-history of the malaria-carrying mosquito was not finally unravelled till just before the end of the last century. The man largely responsible for this research was a Scottish doctor, Sir Ronald Ross, who carried out experiments for many years in India. War has been waged on the mosquito ever since, and in recent years success has been growing rapidly.

Two main methods of attack have been developed. The first, which is particularly important in areas where towns exist, is to destroy the mosquito by spraying the inside of houses regularly with insecticides such as D.D.T. In addition, nearby marshes may be drained, and oil is spread over any other likely breeding-grounds to kill the larvae. The second way has been to find new drugs which not only cure the disease but which, if taken regularly, will prevent people from being infected. Some of these are extremely effective.

But over a vast continent like Africa, with so many suitable breeding-places for the mosquito, and so many people suffering from the disease to act as 'reservoirs' from which the disease can be spread, the war is likely to be long and costly. Only small regions, mostly in closely settled parts such as towns, have been cleared. But the change for the better in the last few years is astounding, and provides a hopeful sign for the future.

An exercise in summary writing

9 The following passage is taken from an article dealing with changes in village life. *Using only the information given in the passage,* make a summary, consisting of **two** paragraphs as follows:

a) the social structure of village life in the past;
b) the pattern of village life today.

Select the material you need and arrange it in a sensible order within the appropriate paragraph. *Write in clear and correct English.* Some words and expressions cannot be accurately and economically replaced, but do not copy out long expressions or whole sentences; *use your own words as far as possible.*

Your whole summary should not exceed 150 words altogether; at the end of your work state the exact number of words you have used.

Perhaps one of the reasons underlying the success of 'The Archers' as a popular radio serial is that the everyday picture of country life which it presents takes some account of the fact that the world of the village evolves gradually; its changes are rarely sudden or dramatic but they are relentless and irresistible.

The social structure of the English village, even half a

century or so ago, was clearly defined and established according to an easily understood hierarchy based on position or occupation. At the head was the squire or the aristocratic inhabitant of the 'great house'. Then there came a miscellaneous group of gentry, often retired and sometimes relatives of landed families in the county; in this group the village parson must be included. There followed in the scheme of things the large farmers and below them the school teacher, the farm bailiff, the shop-keepers, and certain skilled craftsmen. Finally there were the smallholders and then the workers who had their own occupational prestige scale according to their jobs: shepherd, ploughman, cowman, pig-keeper, and farm-hand.

The 'great house' and its family was no doubt an object of respect and a source of bounty. Deference was demanded – and received – from tenants and cottagers whose livelihood was partly dependent on the goodwill of the owner. Many of the working-class laboured on the estate or in the house itself and this dependence inculcated attitudes of respect. The aristocrat and his family were often completely ignorant of local affairs and surrounded by hangers-on. Today, however, the squire is more likely to be sitting on the magistrates' bench and aware of the social problems that help to cause delinquency or, as a member of the local council, taking an active interest in housing the poor, providing better social amenities, or offering services to the aged. His own social position, nevertheless, is being challenged in today's changing world.

The parson is still there but his position, too, has altered. He has to look after many parishes and his former lucrative living is no longer comfortable as inflation grows and his benefice remains constant. He cannot rely on his former status or income as a rector or vicar and finds it impossible to maintain much of an appearance in the community, as he crouches in an enormous rectory, helps his wife with the washing-up, and worries about the cost of heating and cleaning such a vast mansion.

The changing life of the village is perhaps best reflected in the life of the farm-worker. His improved general education, his higher wages negotiated by a powerful trade union, his working hours that are permanently fixed, and his more humane conditions of service reveal a different attitude towards the lot of the labourer. Not so long ago he was expected to live in sub-standard housing, accept depressed wages as his lot, and, without thought of changing employment, devote the whole of his life and energies to the needs of one farm, where he counted himself fortunate to be employed. Hours of work were not reckoned, holidays were neither offered nor expected, and machines were not available to relieve him of drudgery. Cows had to be milked; sheep were not clock-watchers in the lambing season; and a fine light evening could not be idly spent when there was a harvest to be brought in. Today the farm-worker has a standard working-week beyond which he calculates his overtime as readily and easily as the factory-worker on a car-production line.

(For further exercises see B. Rowe and R. A. Banks, *Twenty Summaries in English Language for GCE*, 1974, Hodder and Stoughton.)

An exercise in summary and directed writing

10 The passage below deals with certain aspects of vandalism. Using only the material contained in this passage write an article, in *two* paragraphs, for your local newspaper, setting out:

a) the serious effects of vandalism;
b) the possible causes of vandalism.

Your two paragraphs should correspond to (a) and (b) above. *Do not add ideas of your own* but select and arrange material from the passage. *Write in good, clear, accurate English and use an appropriate style.* Your article should be in your own words as far as possible; do not copy out whole sentences or expressions.
  Your final article should not exceed 175 words altogether; at the end state the exact number of words you have used.

A feature of the last twenty years has been the rapid increase in vandalism in Britain. Vandalism itself, however, is not a new phenomenon, since through the ages there have always been those who preferred to destroy rather than to create; even the word 'vandalism' owes its origin to a race of barbarians who devastated parts of Europe as long ago as the fifth century.
  The mis-spelt graffiti, uprooted newly-planted trees, abused train carriages, smashed phone boxes, and bus-stop shelters recklessly destroyed spoil the environment and deprive the public of their amenities for which they have paid. Those who perpetrate such outrages seem to be without any self-discipline and show scant respect for the rights of their fellow-citizens. Moreover, they increase the taxes and the rates that they themselves will have to pay.
  Some argue that the vandals feel rejected by society with its predominant middle-class standards and have far too much

time on their hands. It is conceivable that poor housing and squalid living conditions may lead to this anti-social behaviour, but, if these are the principal causes, it needs to be explained why most of the socially deprived are not vandals. One thing is certain: in order to repair the damage done, local rates have to be increased and national levels of income tax have to take account of the increased expenditure needed to maintain services. Scarce material resources and human skills are unnecessarily wasted in the attempts to reduce the danger to life and property caused by vandalism.

Those who practise vandalism are often of poor education and without parental control. They would defend their behaviour, perhaps, by arguing that society provides them with few youth clubs and recreational activities and that they have nothing better to do with their time. The truth is that they are insecure and feel they must put on a show of bravado in order to impress their peers and members of the gang. Perhaps the growth of gangs and movements such as the punks, mods, and greasers, has played a major rôle in the increase in vandalism.

It is a pity that the development of new schools and improved health services has been jeopardised because of a lack of financial resources when these very resources are being squandered in repairing the damage and making good the destruction caused by vandalism. The situation poses a real challenge to those responsible for educating the young or maintaining law and order. The evidence everywhere of vandalism demeans the standing of the country in the eyes of foreign visitors who are amazed to read the obscene remarks scrawled illiterately across walls or step through the broken glass of street lamps smashed 'just for a joke'. The pride, too, of local people in their environment is being eroded.

Some of the socially-minded politicians give up their efforts to improve the quality of life in the face of such mindless destruction; imaginative designers and developers are reduced to designing amenities which are vandal-proof rather than beautiful and attractive. The older generation, with some justification, blames the younger one and age-groups become even more sharply divided. Some local authorities have become reluctant to improve recreational and social facilities because of vandalism, which is aided and abetted, it is sometimes suggested, by the reduction in police surveillance and an apparently uninterested public which looks the other way when it sees vandals at work. Too many are content to blame the invention of the aerosol can and the felt-tip pen, which make it easy to vandalise buildings and other people's property. Ostrich-like, many ignore what they see and hope that the trail of devastation will cease with the coming of a new generation.

(For a further discussion of this kind of exercise and more passages to work see R. A. Banks and F. D. A. Burns, *Summary and Directed Writing*, Hodder and Stoughton, 1980; and R. A. Banks, *Living English*, Hodder and Stoughton, 1983.)

11 Read the following passage carefully. What fallacies can you find in its argument?

'In *that* direction,' the Cat said, waving its right paw round, 'lives a Hatter; and in *that* direction,' waving the other paw, 'lives a March Hare. Visit either you like: they're both mad.'

'But I don't want to go among mad people,' Alice remarked.

'Oh, you can't help that,' said the Cat: 'we're all mad here. I'm mad. You're mad.'

'How do you know I'm mad?' said Alice.

'You must be,' said the Cat, 'or you wouldn't have come here.'

Alice didn't think that proved it at all. However, she went on: 'And how do you know that you're mad?'

'To begin with,' said the Cat, 'a dog's not mad. You grant that?'

'I suppose so,' said Alice.

'Well, then,' the Cat went on, 'you see a dog growls when its angry, and wags its tail when it's pleased. Now *I* growl when I'm pleased and wag my tail when I'm angry. Therefore I'm mad.'

In **Chapter 9** (pp. 124–37) it was shown that reading is an active occupation; the reader will respond to signs, advertisements, newspapers, and poetry according to his or her own nature, outlook on life, and experience.

The reason for reading will also condition response. Most of us will be making decisions as we read about what is relevant and what is irrelevant for us, about whether we are interested or not interested, about whether the text is clear and helpful or confused and misleading. We sometimes read for a serious purpose and sometimes to be entertained and amused. These are some of the factors which will determine *how* we read.

Speed-reading

The speed at which you read will depend particularly on your purpose for reading and the difficulty of the material. Imagine that you live in Ashford in Middlesex and you are looking for a cycle shop in your area. How long would it take you to find such a shop from the following extract from the *Yellow Pages* British Telecom Directory?

10.1

◆ Cycle shops

Alpha cycles, 94 Cathedral St,
SW19 .... 076 729
Aston Cycles and Electricals,
33 Hexley Rd, SW19 .... 058 470
Barton, N.F. (Cycles), 25 Entworth St 079 439
Basley, R.P., 93 Holiday Ave, Feltham 072 882
Bexworth Cycles, 327 High St, Addlestone 728 000
Bicycles Inc, 2 Bentworth Rd 059 065
Boston Frames, 22 The Groves, W. Byfleet 024 368
Bretts Cycles, 93 Hilton Ave, Hampton 1H   060 125
By-Cycle, 294 The Dale, Tolworth 060 982
Chatsworth Wheels, 23 Pendleby Cres,
Chertsey 023 588
Clamps, 296 Vernon Dr, Molesey
.... **Walton-on-T** 280 005
Cycles Galore (UK) Ltd, 3 Breaks La, Southall... **063
528**
Danton's, 2 Gear La, SW6 .... 074 783

Denning Cycles, 315 Watersplash Rd,
Teddington 085 884
East Rd Cycles, 2 East Rd, W5 .... 050 982
Entertainment Cycles, 31 The Parade,
Sutton 079 589
Flyaway Bicycles, 22 Rollover Rd, Surbiton 024 359

GRANTHAMS LTD—
4 Hydes La, Peckham 012 468
37 The Broadway, Worcester Pk 246 800
296 Rightson Rd, Hounslow 077 785
2 The Main Drive, New Malden 056 283
186 The Dene, Sutton 082 286
27 Bishop's Way, W6 .... 098 370
Wideacres, Morden 084 787
73 Old Ford Rd, W5 .... 098 122
60 Endsleigh Hill Rd, SW15 .... 042 482
90 Market Hill, Ewell 020 630
29 Tyreburst Hill, Surbiton 058 472
6 Drive-off Ave, New Cross 036 553

Handlebars (Cycles) Ltd, 1 Eastcheap,
   Mitcham **246**8094
Hawsworth, N.F., 75 Chestnut Rd,
   Claygate...**728**008
Heads Cycle Centre, 2 Wentworth La,
   Hounslow...**246**8888
Henton, A.J., 9 Easy Way, Ashford...........**246**8031
Hurns (Cycles) Ltd, Hd Off,
   71 Upper Chepe St, SW15.....................**038**987
Jackmans Cycle Centre,
   32 Wry La, Whitton, Twickenham **065**887
Junipers Cycles, 395 The Ditch**Walton-on-T** 28 034
Kemsley, E.B. & Son, 174 The Drive,
   Brentford..**036**288
K Z Sports and Cycles, 95 Highway Rd,
   SW20..**099**286
Lex Cycle Centre, 2 Sutton Parade, Sutton **074**372
Maslen, R.E., 74 Brent La, Hayes................**094**684
Model Bikes, 395 Rollup Rd, Hayes **079**726
Mustins, 6 The Grove, Fulham, SW6...........**076**686
Newtime Bikes, The Rectory La,
   Twickenham...**044**378
Oxbridge Cycles, Manship Ave,
   Oxshott **03722**99375
Peggyls, 9 The Highway, Richmond...........**036**581

PENSWORTH CYCLE CENTRE
75 The Marshes, E Molesey **044**582

Puddle Cycles Ltd, 24 Rose Crescent,
   Sutton **026**373
Puxton, J.F., 29 Silver La, SW6 ....**045**421
Quest Cycles, 86 Hospital Rise, SW19........**053**021
Rise Bikes Ltd, 52 Coin Rd, Richmond **084**663
Riverside Cycle Centre, 22 Malden Way **036**586

RON'S BIKES LTD
Repairs/Accessories ETC
33 Hideaway Rd, Leatherhead...................**026**288
Rowton Wheels, 73 Saddle Rd, Hayes........**044**285
Rudge, F.K. & Sons, 95 Harley Rd,
   Hounslow...**050**277
Sawleys Cycle Centre, 2 Municipal Rd,
   Feltham...01-**246** 8034
Sextons, The Avenue, Wimbledon, SW19   **054**685
Thimbles Cycle Shop, 7 Riverway Dr,
   Kington-upon-Thames **044**588
Victors Value Velocipedes, 72 Rye La, SE9 **078**579
Wandsley, R.K.,
   31 Rogues Rd,....................**Walton-on-T** 280093
Wardoff Danger Cycles Ltd,
   32 Entomology Rd, SW19 ....**026**585
Wexford Bikes, 9476 The Hill, Richmond **032**483
Wobbles Ltd, 6 The Bridge Parade.............**090**722
Worths, 71 Handlebar La, W4 ....**027**974

How did you set about finding the information?

Skimming

10.2

There is little point in reading fast unless what is read is understood. It is helpful, in considering how to increase our speed in writing and understanding, to realise the way most people read texts quickly.

Some schemes for teaching children to read depend on building up the shape of a word to the point where it is recognised and then moving on to the next word where the process is repeated. Reading with understanding, however, depends on grouping words into units of sense and only the experience of reading many texts will allow a child to recognise quickly the way a sentence breaks down into such units. To show how important such a recognition is for fast, smooth reading, try to read aloud the following passage which keeps to normal spelling of words but reverses the order in which English is normally printed (from left to right, to right to left instead).

   ym dna ,pirriP gnieb eman ylimaf s'rehtaf yM
   eugnot tnafni ym ,pilihP eman naitsirhc
   ro regnol gnihton seman htob fo ekam dluoc

dellac I ,oS .piP naht ticilpxe erom
.piP dellac eb ot emac dna ,piP flesym
(Opening of Charles Dickens's *Great Expectations*.)

Swift reading can take place once the skill in spotting the way a sentence breaks down into units of meaning has been acquired. The eye then picks up the key word(s) in each unit and makes its own connections between them. Decide, for example, the meaning of the following:

10.3

> . . . Green Cross Code . . . guide . . . pedestrians. . . . children . . . taught . . . not be allowed . . . until . . . understand and apply it. The age . . . will vary . . . many children under seven cannot . . . understand . . . apply . . . parts of the code . . . judgement of the speed and distance of . . . vehicles. Teaching children the code . . . must . . . suited to each individual child.

Had the words omitted, however, been those given, the passage would have been impossible to follow:

> The . . . is a . . . for all. However . . . need to be . . . how to use it and should . . . out alone . . . they can. . . . at which they can do this . . .; for instance, . . . fully . . . and . . . those . . . requiring . . . approaching. and the age at which parents allow them to go out and cross roads by themselves . . . therefore be . . .

The *fastest* readers sometimes fix their eyes on the centre of each line and allow their sight to pick up a word or two each side of the point at which they are looking. They then run their eyes straight down the centre of the page and make connections between the 'key' words picked up. Such reading, of course, does not lead to *accurate* reading and cannot be used in situations where the details are of crucial significance – as in recipes or car workshop manuals. Such speed-reading, however, is a useful skill to acquire if the time available for surveying a range of text books is limited; such reading will allow a student to recognise which passages will be worth further, close attention.

10.4

Close reading

A different technique is required for close reading, since it demands careful consideration of viewpoint, topic, context, and intended audience. Levels of meaning, ordering of the material, and the contextual meaning of individual words will need to be considered by the reader who is attempting to understand in depth. Comprehension

10.5

exercises in examinations demand such reading – as does the small print of insurance policies or the clauses in a legal agreement. Notice how closely you need to read the following passage from a recent examination in order to answer the questions which follow:

A small boy stood in the doorway of a wine shop, thin, barefooted, with short and scruffy hair. The girl with him also had cropped hair, so that her head looked as though it were covered with scorched grass; she was about eleven years old, but her dark slanting eyes were as quick and frisky as fish. The boy had come   5
to sing. He screwed himself up and sang in a high passionate wail, throbbing, trembling, tearing his heart out. He seemed to be singing himself to death, as though each song was a paroxysm which diminished and bled his frail young body. And while he sang the girl perpetually watched him, anxious and maternal,   10
echoing each phrase of his song with mute contortions of her lips. Afterwards she took him by the hand and led him round, charming us all for alms. But they preferred to be paid in monkey-nuts, which they could eat.

The night before we left Seville I walked late in the streets   15
alone. As I headed at last for home I ran suddenly into a gang of carol-singers. They were sitting in an alley, warming their bare feet around a fire of burning paper. When I called to them, they came crowding around me squealing like starlings, grinning and arranging themselves in order. Their leader, a boy of ten, mut-   20
tered a few instructions. Then they sang me five ecstatic carols, their smiles wiped away, their faces set in a kind of soft unconscious rapture. Here again, as in the others I had heard, was the same order, expertness and love. A girl of five took a solo, singing through the short tangles of her hair in a voice of such hoarse   25
sweetness one felt shriven of all one's sins.

1 The description of the boy in the first sentence (lines 1–2) suggests that he was all the following EXCEPT
   A   unkempt
   B   poor
   C   underfed
   D   neglected
   E   unhappy

2 Which one of the following words is closest in meaning to 'perpetually' as used in line 10?
   A   Intently
   B   Unceasingly
   C   Repeatedly
   D   Untiringly
   E   Intermittently

3 The contortions of the girl's lips are described as 'mute' (line 11) because she was
  A mouthing the words silently
  B singing softly to herself
  C trying to recall the words
  D giving the boy moral support
  E providing an accompaniment

4 According to the first paragraph (lines 1–14), all the following can be inferred about the girl EXCEPT that she
  A appeared to be alert and observant
  B was not shy of approaching strangers
  C felt protective towards the boy
  D was unable to sing herself
  E knew what the boy's performance would be

5 The singers' smiles were 'wiped away' (line 22) most probably because the children were
  A dominated by their leader
  B taking their singing seriously
  C going off into raptures
  D feeling a little embarrassed
  E trying to earn money

6 Which one of the following words is closest in meaning to 'rapture' as used in line 23?
  A Tranquillity
  B Detachment
  C Seriousness
  D Excitement
  E Transport

7 According to the second paragraph (lines 15–26) the carol-singers sang with all the following EXCEPT
  A delight
  B intensity
  C skill
  D melancholy
  E concord

8 From the passage as a whole, all the following statements about the writer can be inferred EXCEPT that he
  A was moved by singing
  B appreciated a good performance
  C was a keen observer
  D felt guilty before such poverty
  E was fond of children

Exercises

1 Read the following extract first at speed and then more slowly in order to discover what point the writer was trying to make. (There are a number of clues.)

> In a column in a newspaper there was a Union advertisement of a picture of a railwayman looking like a consumptive in the last stages, and embracing one of his horrible children, while his more horrible wife and mother supported the feeble heads of others, and under it was written, 'Is this man an anarchist? He wants a wage to keep his family', and it was awful to think that he and his family would perhaps get the wage and be kept after all. The question about whether he was an anarchist was obviously unanswerable without further data, as there was nothing in the picture to show his political convictions; they might, from anything that appeared, have been Liberal, Tory, Labour, Socialist, Anarchist or Coalition-Unionist. And anyhow, supposing that he had been an anarchist, he would still, presumably, have wanted a wage to keep his family. Anarchists are people who disapprove of authority, not of wages. The member of the Union who composed that picture must have had a muddled mind.

Did you notice any differences in the speed and in the way you read this extract from the way you read the list of cycle shops in the *Yellow Pages* on pp. 147–8. Can you explain why there were any such differences?

2 Rewrite the following passages from *The Highway Code* inserting words where there are dashes. (The context should enable you to make most of the correct choices.)

    a) – are dual-carriageway roads – – not – – by pedestrians, learner –, –, and riders of small motorcycles. Slow-moving –, agricultural –, and some – used by invalids are also –, – – – offence to pick up or – – – passenger or – – on any part of – –.

    b) When you – a motorway other than – – –, you will approach from – – on the left (– – –). Give way to – already – – –. Watch for – suitable – in the traffic in the left-hand – on the – and then adjust your – in the extra lane so that when you join it you are already travelling – – – –. If there is not a suitable –, – in the – – until it is safe to – – –.

Comprehension

3 Read the passage carefully and then answer the questions. Each question has five suggested answers. Select the best answer to each question.

At five years old, my mother took me to my first play. Clearly I remember that it was a matinee about Nero, fiddling madly before the burning of Rome. A deafening thunderstorm went on in the background, through which Nero's mother, Agrippi-
5   na, shrieked valedictions to her insensitive son. Alternately, the stage glowed red from the flames consuming Rome, or was blacked out altogether while the thunder lasted, or flared white with the lightning. Through all these extremes of heat and shade and light I clung to my mother, protesting loudly that I
10 was not frightened. Our other guest, Hedworth Williamson, appeared to treat the appalling scene in front of him with comforting levity, however, and gradually I too began to scoff at it as being 'only a play'.
In the row behind us a lady arrived late. At that moment the
15 stage was at its blackest and the thunder at its most loud. Blindly, she groped her way into her seat. Then she took the long pins out of her hat, removed her hat and pinned it to the back of the seat in front of her. A scream, not from Agrippina, rang out by my side. On the stage the lightning flared, and by
20 its light I beheld the terrifying spectacle of Hedworth William-son impaled, like a gigantic butterfly, on the back of his seat. And a doctor had to be sent for to dress the wound and to treat him for shock.
Needless to say, the psychiastrist added this episode to my
25 first important impressions. And, inevitably, from it I derived a lifelong fear of thunder and lightning, and a dream-ridden fear of being stabbed in the back.
Very carefully, my mother chose my next play: 'Mother Goose'.

I Which one of the following is closest in meaning to 'alternately' as used in line 5?
  A Alternatively
  B By chance
  C Fluctuatingly
  D By turns
  E Periodically

II The child's early reaction to the play (lines 8–10) was all the following EXCEPT
  A inconsistent
  B serious
  C emotional
  D uninterested
  E afraid

III Which one of the following words is closest in meaning to 'appalling' as used in line 11?
  A Gripping
  B Badly-acted
  C Excruciating
  D Heart-rending
  E Terrifying

IV It can be inferred that the mother's reasons for choosing 'Mother Goose' (lines 28–9) included all the following EXCEPT that it was
  A unlikely to have storm effects
  B not a matinee
  C unlikely to have screams and shrieks
  D not a tragedy
  E unlikely to frighten a child

V All of the following statements can be justified from the passage EXCEPT that
  A the mother's choice for the child's first play was unsuitable
  B the narrator was not frightened by the play
  C Hedworth Williamson did not take the play seriously
  D the performance was often dimly-lit and noisy
  E Nero did not seem to care about Rome's fate

VI The narrator now appears to regard the episode from her childhood mainly with
  A amusement
  B detachment
  C fear
  D nostalgia
  E resentment

(For further examples of comprehension exercises testing inference, vocabulary, imagery, idiom, and summary, and those using different types of multiple-choice items see R. A. Banks, *Don't Guess*, 1985, B. Rowe and R. A. Banks, *Objective Tests in English Language for GCE*, 2nd Ed., 1971, and *New Objective Tests in English Language*, 1974, Hodder and Stoughton.)

4 Read the passage carefully; then answer the questions.

At the close of a December evening when the roads are like
slugs, oozy and gleaming in the cold, two workless and sodden
men were shambling along, lost in the side lanes of silent
country. The houses with their yellow dabs of light had
5   scattered and thinned away. Blistered and squelching and
gone past the cravings of hunger into a hunched, mechanical
misery, the two men went on. It was their third day on the road,
and, no longer exchanging any words, cursing the lanes which
had snared them into homeless, foodless darkness, they
10   seemed to be groping round and round in a pit. Now, they
would almost sooner have found a main road than a plate of
beef.

Suddenly the old one, who was ahead, stopped dead and
then broke into a weak, gasping hobble.
15   "Ere y'are,' he called.

Without warning, after a sudden rise, the lane had finished.
They stood upon a main road. Straight as a dull sword it carved
the country in two, lightless, soundless, without signposts. And
now the two men were appalled. Which way? After the
20   winding roads, this great one seemed to strike them like a plank
flat in the face. It jerked the knees in their sockets. It was as hard
as iron to the weak bones.

On this third day the object of their journey had been driven
from their minds altogether. They did not care if they never got
25   to the town where the factory and the jobs were said to be. They
had eaten poorly on the first two days when the adventure was
young, but on this day the singing had stopped and the
whistling. The only sounds all days had been the dazed singing
in their heads, the gritting of their teeth.
30   During the daytime, neither work nor towns but food had
been their only thought. They ached and craved for it. Every
step was for food, every glance sharpened the search for it,
every sound was passed in judgment, every sight was questioned. The anarchy of hunger was in their bubbling bellies
35   which blew weakly out or cavernously sank.

I For which *two* of the following reasons are the roads compared to slugs (lines 1–2)?

> **1** The men moved slowly along them.
> **2** They had wet and slimy surfaces.
> **3** The men's feet squelched on them.
> **4** They were shiny in the evening light.

> **A** **1** and **2** only
> **B** **1** and **3** only
> **C** **2** and **3** only
> **D** **2** and **4** only
> **E** **3** and **4** only

II Which one of the following words is closest in meaning to 'sodden' as used in line 2?

> **A** Dirty
> **B** Melancholy
> **C** Wretched
> **D** Exhausted
> **E** Soaked

III Which *three* of the following statements can be deduced from the sentence beginning 'The houses . . .' (lines 2–3)?

> **1** The houses they now passed were all small and shabby.
> **2** It had been dark for some time.
> **3** There were now hardly any houses near the lanes.
> **4** The country people had all gone to bed.
> **5** The men had earlier passed through a more populous area.

> **A** **1**, **2** and **4** only
> **B** **1**, **2** and **5** only
> **C** **1**, **3** and **4** only
> **D** **2**, **3** and **5** only
> **E** **3**, **4** and **5** only

IV Which *two* of the following are suggested by the reference to the men's misery as 'mechanical' (line 6)?
  1 The physical effort of moving their limbs was painful.
  2 They were hardly conscious of what they were doing.
  3 Their legs kept moving on with monotonous regularity.
  4 They had almost passed beyond feelings of tiredness.
  5 The jolting of their steps vibrated throughout their bodies.

  A **1** and **2** only
  B **1** and **5** only
  C **2** and **3** only
  D **3** and **4** only
  E **4** and **5** only

V Which one of the following words is closest in meaning to 'snared' as used in line 9?
  A Tricked
  B Enticed
  C Ambushed
  D Decoyed
  E Trapped

VI 'They seemed to be groping round and round in a pit' (lines 9–10) for all the following reasons EXCEPT that they
  A seemed to be getting nowhere
  B could see no houses near them
  C had lost all sense of direction
  D felt as if they were trapped
  E were moving in near darkness

VII The men 'would almost sooner have found a main road than a plate of beef' (lines 11–12) because they were
  A lonely
  B workless
  C hungry
  D homeless
  E lost

VIII According to the first paragraph (lines 1–12), the two men were all the following EXCEPT
  A exhausted
  B frustrated
  C aimless
  D wretched
  E uncommunicative

IX The lane seemed to finish 'without warning' (line 16) probably because

    A the men were walking with heads hanging down

    B there were no sign-posts in the side lanes

    C the junction was hidden by a sharp incline

    D it was too dark to see where they were going

    E the main road was round a sudden bend

X Which one of the following words is closest in meaning to 'appalled' as used in line 19?

    A Dismayed

    B Apprehensive

    C Frustrated

    D Indecisive

    E Bewildered

XI According to the passage, the side lanes were all the following EXCEPT

    A wet

    B twisting

    C unlit

    D endless

    E shiny

XII All the following are said of the two men EXCEPT that they were

    A wandering aimlessly

    B out of work

    C soaking wet

    D different in age

    E worn out

XIII Which one of the following clearly shows that the first paragraph (lines 1–12) refers to a later period than that of the last paragraph (lines 30–35)?

    A 'lost in the side lanes of silent country' (lines 3–4)

    B 'The houses . . . had scattered and thinned away' (lines 4–5)

    C 'gone past the cravings of hunger' (line 6)

    D 'their third day on the road' (line 7)

    E 'no longer exchanging any words' (line 8)

Keys to Exercises

Chapter 6, Exercise 15

a) Edith Cavell. Last words, 12 October 1918.
b) Charles Reade 1814–84: recipe for writing novels in serial form.
c) Edward Lear 1812–88: To make an Amblongus Pie.
d) Attributed to Rev. W. A. Spooner, 1844–1930: a 'spoonerism'.
e) W. Keble Martin, *The Concise British Flora in Colour,* Sphere Books, 1965, plate 53; the Dandelion.
f) A primary school classroom where remedial reading classes are conducted. A 'No Comment' Feature in *The Times Educational Supplement,* 19 August 1983.
g) Accident report to an insurance company.
h) *The Highway Code,* HMSO, 1978, p. 9.
i) Opening sentence of Jane Austen, *Pride and Prejudice.*
j) Letter to a Social Security Office.

Chapter 9, Exercise 6
a) 41¼ hours; b) £107; c) There was only one outward bus per week and this had arrived from London on Friday at 10.30 and was returning to London the same day; d) £550.

Chapter 10, pages 00–00
Keys: E, B, A, D, B, E, D, D.

Chapter 10, Exercise 2

a) Motorways . . . which must . . . be used . . . drivers, cyclists . . . vehicles . . . vehicles . . . carriages . . . prohibited. It is an . . . set down a . . . a hitch-hiker . . . the motorway.
b) . . . join . . . at its start . . . a road . . . (a slip road) . . . traffic . . . on the motorway . . . a . . . gap . . . lane . . . motorway . . . speed . . . at the same speed . . . gap, wait . . . acceleration lane . . . enter the motorway.

Chapter 10, Exercise 3
Keys: D, D, E, B, B, A.

Chapter 10, Exercise 4
Keys: D, E, D, C, E; B, E, C, C, A; D, A, C.

Index

Bold type indicates a main entry